LANG
BOOK PUBLISHING

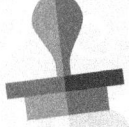

Children's Torah

Activity Book 3

By Belinda McCallion

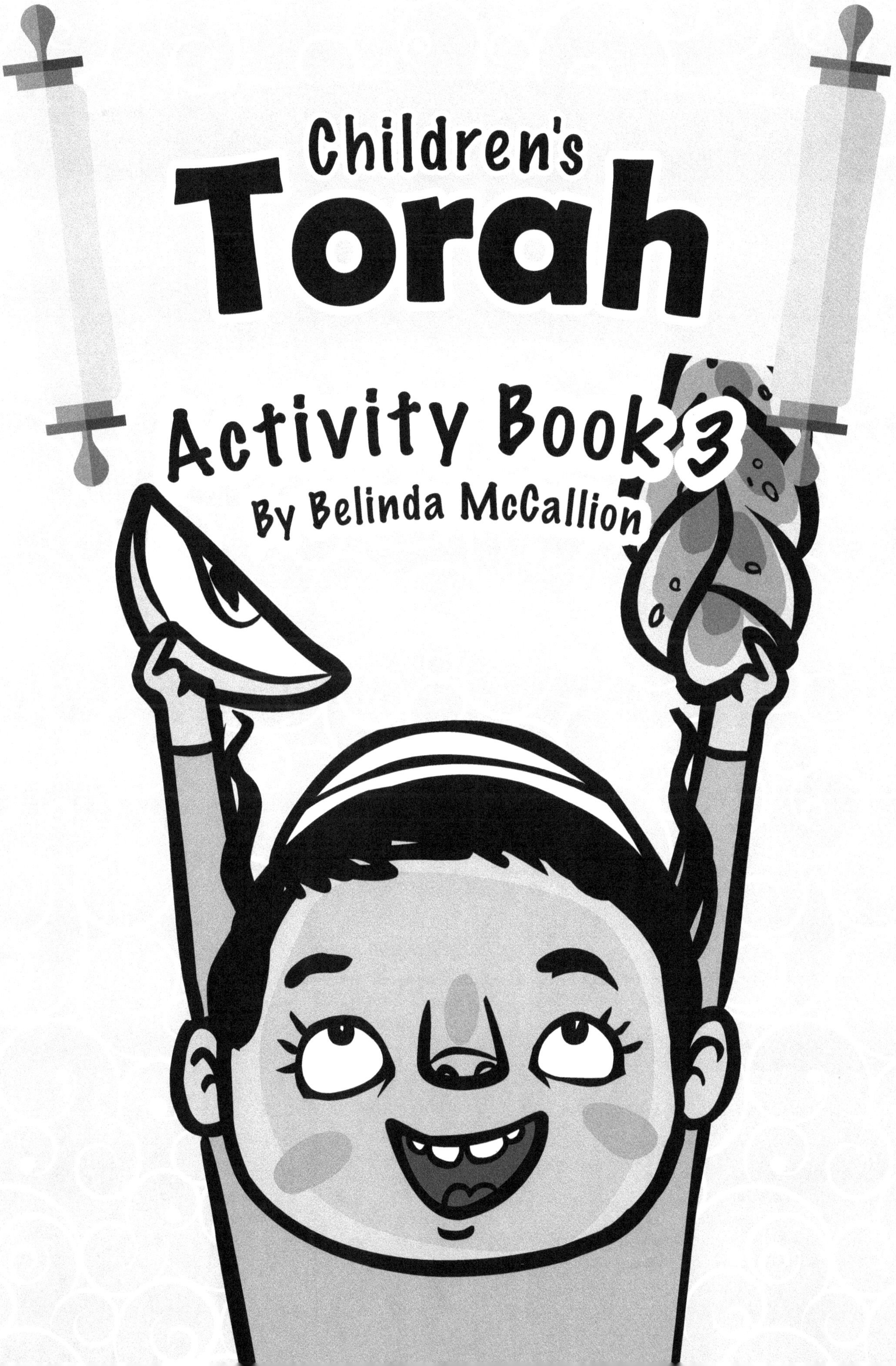

langbookpublishing.com

No part of this book may be reproduced, stored in a retrieval system, or transmitted by any means, electronic, mechanical, photocopying, recording, or otherwise without written permission from the author.

Copyright © Belinda McCallion 2017. All rights reserved.

The right of Belinda McCallion to be identified as author of the Work has been asserted by her in accordance with the New Zealand Copyright Act 1994.

National Library of New Zealand Cataloguing-in-Publication Data
Lang Book Publishing 2017

Co-edited by J. M. Betham-Lang and Roger Lang
Cover design by Blair McLean

ISBN 978-0-9941422-7-6

Published in New Zealand
A catalogue record for this book is available from the National Library of New Zealand.
Kei te pātengi raraunga o Te Puna Mātauranga o Aotearoa te whakarārangi o tēnei pukapuka.

This book Belongs to:

_____

How to use this book:

These worksheets have been especially designed for easy photocopy duplication.

Each lesson has 3 parts; a Torah, a Haftara and a B'rit Hadashah.

The main page of each part is the instruction page. This is not intended to replace the actual reading of the portion but to be a tool that can be used to summarise the readings and find a few key messages from the readings.

The activity page relates to the lesson and is intended to be used to reinforce the messages. This page caters to a wide age group, as there is always a picture to colour and a more difficult activity. Each activity sheet ranges in difficulty level dependent on the lesson. There is an answer page at the back of the book if you get stuck.

Table of Contents

Lesson 24

Parasha 24 Vayikra (Leviticus 1:1-5:26) 2

Haftara 24 Yeshayahu (Isaiah 43:21-44:23) 4

B'rit Hadashah 24 (John 1:19-37) 6

Lesson 25

Parasha 25 Tzav Vayikra (Leviticus 6:1-8:36) 8

Haftara 25 Yirmeyahu (Jeremiah 7:21-8:3;9:22-23) . . 10

B'rit Hadashah 25 (Acts 13:1-5) 12

Lesson 26

Parasha 26 Sh'mini Vayikra (Leviticus 9:1-11:47) . . . 14

Haftara 26 Sh'muel Bet (2 Samuel 6:1-19) 16

B'rit Hadashah 26 (Acts 10) 18

Lesson 27

Parasha 27 Tazria Vayikra (Leviticus 12:1-13:59) 20

Haftara 27 Melakhim Bet (2 Kings 4:42-5:19) 22

B'rit Hadashah 27 (Luke 5:12-15) 24

Lesson 28

Parasha 28 Metzorah Vayikra (Leviticus 14:1-15:33) . . 26

Haftara 28 Melakim Bet (2 Kings 7:3-20) 28

B'rit Hadashah 28 (Luke 8:43-48) 30

Lesson 29

Parasha 29 Acrei Mot Vayikra (Leviticus 16:1-18:30) . . 32

Haftara 29 Yirmeyahu (Ezekiel 22:1-19) 34

B'rit Hadashah 29 (Hebrews 9:1-26) 36

Lesson 30

Parasha 30 Kedoshim Vayikra (Leviticus 19:1-20:27) . 38

Haftara 30 Yachezk'el (Ezekiel 20:2-20) 40

B'rit Hadashah 30 (Acts 15:1-21) 42

Lesson 31

Parasha 31 Emor Vayikra (Leviticus 21:1-24:23) 44

Haftara 31 Yechezkel (Ezekiel 44:15-31) 46

B'rit Hadashah 31 (Luke 23:53-24:8) 48

Lesson 32

Parasha 32 Behar Vayikra (Leviticus 25:1-26:2) 50

Haftara 32 Yirmeyahu (Jeremiah 32:6-27) 52

B'rit Hadashah 32 (John 8:30-36) 54

Lesson 33

Parasha 33 Bechukotai Vayikra (Leviticus 26:27:34) . . 56

Haftara 33 Yirmeyahu (Jeremiah 16:19-17:14) 58

B'rit Hadashah 33 (John 1:15-21) 60

Special Shabbats

Shabbat Zachor (Purim) 1 Samuel 15:2-34 62

Shabbat Ha Gadol (Pesach) Malachi 3:4-24 64

Extra Pesach lessons 66

Answers 71

References 73

Vayikra

פרשת ויקרא

(He Called) Leviticus 1:1-5:26(6:7)

Parasha 24

Memory Verse

"He is to lay his hand upon the head of the burnt offering and it will be accepted on his behalf to make atonement for him."

Leviticus 1:4 CJB

Did You Know?

The book of Leviticus was said to be written in the year 1440 BC.

STORY SUMMARY

ADONAI Tells the People How to Sacrifice to Him: ADONAI gives provision and instruction for five types of sacrifices-The Burnt Offering, Grain Offering, Peace Offering, Sin Offering and the Guilt Offering.

WORD FOCUS

Korban, Le-hakriv: 'Sacrifice'. This word comes from the word which means to 'come near, to approach or become close in relationship with someone'. Our sin separates us from ADONAI. Ever since sin came into the world, ADONAI has been inviting us to come close to Him again

MAIN MESSAGE

By laying a hand onto the sacrificial animal, it was understood that the sin and guilt of the person offering the sacrifice was being transferred to the innocent animal. Sometimes it was the priests who were to do this on behalf of the people and sometimes the people were to do it directly. Through allowing this system, ADONAI once again showed His unfailing love. Unfortunately sin is ugly and does bring death; however, through ADONAI's provision, there was a way to be close to Him, again, and to have their own lives spared.

PROVISION of ADONAI   **RELATIONSHIP**   **REPENTANCE**

Promise

Psalms 103:8-12 CJB

"ADONAI is merciful and compassionate, slow to anger and rich in grace. He will not always accuse, He will not keep His anger forever, He has not treated us as our sins deserve or paid us back for our offenses, because His mercy toward those who fear Him is far above earth and heaven. He has removed our sin from us as far as the east is from the west."

Vayikra Leviticus 1:1-5:26(6:7) Activity Sheet

Types of Sacrifices

Can you remember the five types of sacrifices?

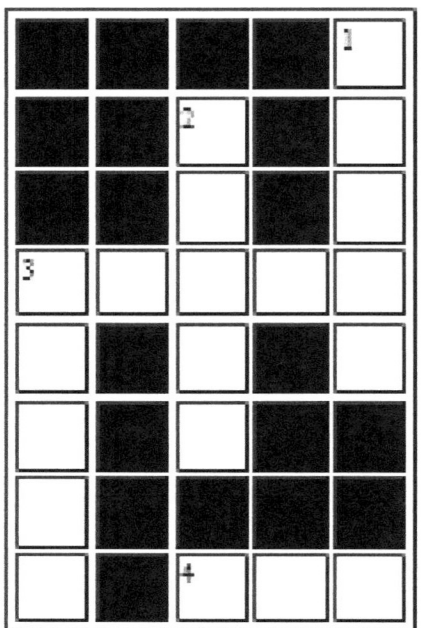

ACROSS

3. _____ Offering Lev 2:1

4. _____ Offering Lev 4:14

DOWN

1. _____ Offering Lev 1:3

2. _____ Offering Lev 3:1

3. _____ Offering Lev 5:6

* Some versions will have different words. For more help see Story Summary on lesson page.

Sin Transfer

"He is to lay his hand upon the head of the burnt offering and it will be accepted on his behalf to make atonement for him."

Leviticus 1:4 CJB

Yesha 'Yahu

Isaiah 43:21-44:23

Haftara 24 (Prophets)

Memory Verse

"Keep these matters in mind, Ya'akov (Jacob), for you, Isra'el, are my servant. I formed you, you are my own servant; Isra'el, don't forget me."

Isaiah 44:21 CJB

Did You Know?

Isaiah's ministry was about 40-60 years.

STORY SUMMARY

ADONAI calls the People to Return: Through Isaiah, ADONAI tells the people how they have forgotten their covenant with Him and have stopped their sacrifices. Then ADONAI reminds them they are a chosen people. He encourages them and gives hope for the future. ADONAI then warns the people of the dangers in choosing a different way and tells the people to come back to Him so He can bless them.

WORD FOCUS

Bachar: 'Chosen'. This word originally meant to 'wall in a flock of sheep'. Isra'el was not chosen to be ADONAI's people just for their own benefit. They were chosen to be a 'wall', a 'light' to the nations and to show the love of ADONAI to the whole world. When Isra'el turned away from ADONAI they also turned away from this great privilege. ADONAI wants us to return to Him so that all people will be blessed.

MAIN MESSAGE

ADONAI is a loving father who is willing and waiting to forgive our sins if we come to Him. If we are not doing His will, we are not fulfilling His plan for us to be a blessing to others. He wants to make us clean and whole so He can use us for His glory. ADONAI does this through encouragement and hope, not by telling us how bad and hopeless we are.

ENCOURAGEMENT **HOPE** **OBEY**

Promise

Isaiah 44:23 CJB

"Sing, you heavens, for ADONAI has done it! Shout, you depths of the earth! Mountains, break out in song, along with every tree in the forest! For ADONAI has redeemed Ya'akov (Jacob); He glorifies Himself in Isra'el."

Yesha Yahu Isaiah 43:21-44:23   Activity Sheet

Come Home to ADONAI

ADONAI wants us to come back to him. He doesn't want it to take a long time. Help this lost Isra'elite find the short cut back to ADONAI.

Willows on the Riverbank

"They will spring up among the grass like willows on the riverbanks." Isaiah 44:4 CJB

John
B'rit Hadashah 24
1:19-37
(Newer Testament)

STORY SUMMARY

Yochanan the Baptist identifies Yeshua: Yochanan has been called by ADONAI to baptise and prepare the way for the Messiah. ADONAI says, "who the spirit lands on is the Messiah." Yochanan sees the spirit land like a dove and remain on Yeshua. He knows that Yeshua is the promised Messiah.

WORD FOCUS

Yochanan: 'ADONAI is gracious'. Through sending Yeshua to the world, ADONAI showed us His grace and mercy.

MEMORY VERSE

"...Look! ADONAI's Lamb! The one who is taking away the sin of the world!" John 1:29 CJB

MAIN MESSAGE

The sacrificial system of the Tanakh pointed to the sacrifice of Yeshua. He was the perfect sacrifice. Everything in the past pointed to Yeshua and His death on our behalf as the sacrificial lamb of ADONAI.

PROMISE

"...'The one on whom you see the spirit descending and remaining, this is the one who immerses in the Ruach Ha Kodesh.'" John 1:33 CJB

DID YOU KNOW?

Yochanan the Baptist lived in the wilderness. He ate locusts and honey and wore camel hair clothing with a leather belt, just as Eliyahu (Elijah) the prophet had worn.

John 1:19-37 Activity Sheet

Lamb of ADONAI

"As soon as Yeshua was immersed, He came up out of the water. At that moment heaven was opened, He saw the spirit of ADONAI coming down upon Him like a dove." Matthew 3:16 CJB

Spirit of ADONAI

Connect this dot to dot to see what the spirit was like when it came down on Yeshua.

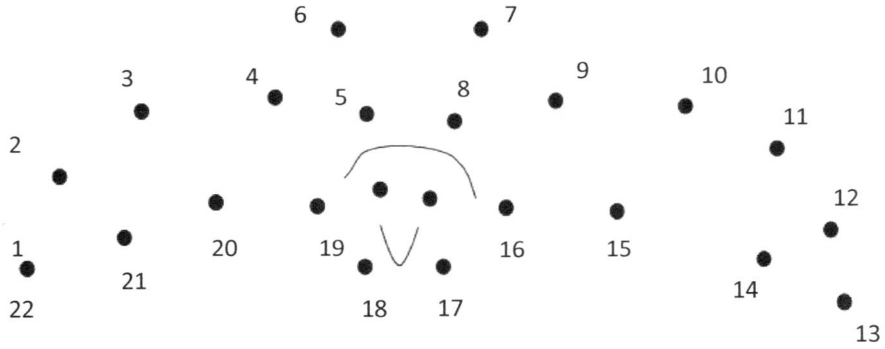

Tzav
פרשת צו

(Give an Order) Leviticus (Vayikra) 6:1-8:36

Parasha 25

Memory Verse

"Fire is to be kept burning on the altar continually; it is not to go out." Leviticus 6:6 CJB

Did You Know?

For the sin offering, they had to destroy the most valuable part. This would be like keeping the box and throwing away the toy. This showed how costly sin was.

STORY SUMMARY

ADONAI Describes the Five Sacrifices: In the last parasha we were introduced to the five sacrifices. Now they are being more fully explained.

Details about the Priests: The priests need to go through a special cleansing process called ordination. ADONAI gives details on exactly how this is to be done.

WORD FOCUS

T'shuvah: 'Return' or 'repent'. The purpose of the sacrifices was to get people to think about their sin and repent. It was about the heart attitude. ADONAI knew His people would not always get things right, no matter how they tried. The sacrifice system made a way for them to stay in connection with Him through true repentance.

MAIN MESSAGE

Each sacrifice had a specific purpose. It was important to ADONAI that His instructions were followed. *The burnt offering* = atonement, *the grain offering* = thanksgiving for the sustenance of life, *the peace offering* = peace with ADONAI, *the sin and guilt offerings* = required blood and was costly.

REPENT   **OBEY**   **BE GRATEFUL**   **BE CLEANSED**   **HAVE HOPE**

Promise

Genesis 8:20-22 CJB

"Noach (Noah) built an altar to *ADONAI*. Then he took every clean animal and every clean bird, and he offered burnt offerings on the altar. *ADONAI* smelled the sweet aroma, and *ADONAI* said in His heart, 'I will never again curse the ground because of humankind...'"

Tzav   Leviticus 6:1-8:36   Activity Sheet

Hebrew Writing

The very first form of the Hebrew language was written in pictures. Each picture had a meaning. The word 'ransom', when seen in pictures, shows the great price that has been paid for us. 'Behold the open door,' How blessed we are to have an open door to ADONAI. What a gift!

From the chart below and the word clues, draw the word '**ransom**'.

Name	Pictograph	Meaning	Name	Pictograph	Meaning
Aleph		Ox / strength / leader	Lamed		Staff / goad / control / "toward"
Bet		House / "In"	Mem		Water / chaos
Gimmel		Foot / camel / pride	Nun		Seed / fish / activity / life
Dalet		Tent door / pathway	Samekh		Hand on staff / support / prop
Hey		Lo! Behold! "The"	Ayin		Eye / to see / experience
Vav		Nail / peg / add / "And"	Pey		Mouth / word / speak
Zayin		Plow / weapon / cut off	Tsade		Man on side / desire / need
Chet		Tent wall / fence / separation	Qof		Sun on horizon / behind
Tet		Basket / snake / surround	Resh		Head / person / first
Yod		Arm and hand / work / deed	Shin		Eat / consume / destroy
Kaf		Palm of hand / to open	Tav		Mark / sign / covenant

Behold	**Tent door**	**See**

Priests

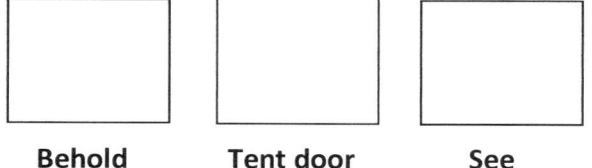

"Aharon and his sons did all the things which *ADONAI* ordered through Moshe." Leviticus 8:36 CJB

Yirmeyahu

Jeremiah 7:21-8:3, 9:22-23

Haftara 25 (Prophets)

Memory Verse

"Here is what ADONAI says: 'The wise man should not boast of his wisdom, the powerful should not boast of his power, the wealthy should not boast of his wealth.'"
Jeremiah 9:23 CJB

Did You Know?

Because of the exiles and the spreading of the Word, ADONAI's children are all over the world today.

STORY SUMMARY

The Children of Isra'el Turn from ADONAI: The people had come to rely on the sacrifice system as the way to please ADONAI. Here ADONAI sets them straight. It is love and obedience which is important, not the sacrifice. ADONAI tried many times to talk to them in the past through messengers such as the prophets, but they wouldn't listen. Now ADONAI is saying, because of their evil ways they will go into exile.

WORD FOCUS

Galut: 'Exile', meaning to 'wander' also to 'discover' or 'reveal'. The purpose of exile was to turn the hearts of the people to home and to reveal ADONAI. He wanted them to be sorry for their sin and return to Him.

MAIN MESSAGE

Although ADONAI wanted the sacrifice system to be followed exactly, the people missed the point. The system was supposed to encourage thankfulness and repentance. The system became too familiar, and they forgot the true meaning of why they were doing it. We also need to serve ADONAI out of a grateful and repentant heart, not just because we have been told to do it.

OBEY   **CONFESS**   **REJOICE**

Promise

Jeremiah 9:24 CJB

"'Instead, let the boaster boast about this: that he understands and knows me - that I am ADONAI, practicing grace, justice and righteousness in the land; for in these things I take pleasure', says ADONAI."

Yirmeyahu Jeremiah 7:21-8:3, 9:22-24 Activity Sheet

The Right Path

As people, we make so many wrong turns. ADONAI wants to be our guide to lead us back home to Him.
Can you find your way through this maze?

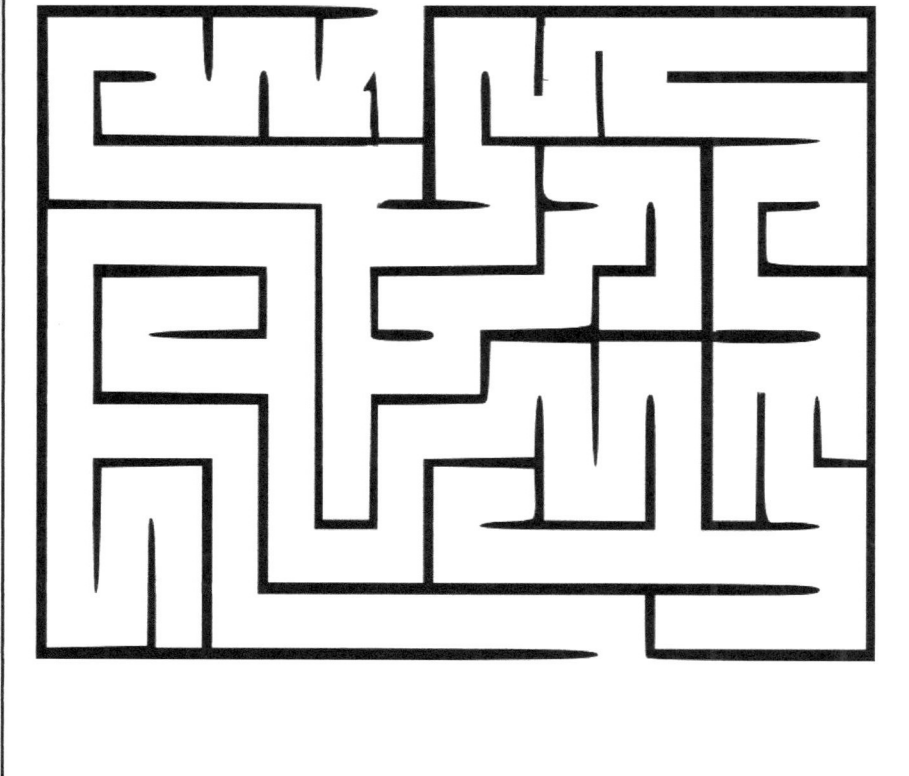

Cranes

"Storks in the sky know their seasons; doves, swallows and cranes their migration times; but my people do not know the rulings of *ADONAI*." Jeremiah 8:7 CJB

B'rit Hadashah 25
(Newer Testament)
Acts 13:1-5

STORY SUMMARY

Ordination of Shaul (Paul) and BarNabba: As the priests were ordained in Leviticus, now ADONAI chooses Shaul and BarNabba (Barnabas) to be ordained or 'set apart'. Their purpose is to bring the good news of Yeshua to wherever they are sent. After their ordination they are sent to Seleucia and then to Cyprus.

WORD FOCUS

Tsom: 'Fast', meaning to cover the mouth or to go without food. When ADONAI's people committed themselves to Him in prayer and fasting, He did amazing things.

MEMORY VERSE

"...Set aside for me BarNabba and Shaul for the work to which I have called them." Acts 13:2 CJB

MAIN MESSAGE

ADONAI chooses different people for different tasks. He sets them apart for His purpose and equips them with what they need to do the work. Just as in the earlier days, ADONAI needs us to be obedient to Him so that His plans can be achieved. Sometimes we prevent the plans of ADONAI by trying to do things our own way and not His way.

PROMISE

"Then, if My people, who bear My name, will humble themselves, pray, seek My face and turn from their evil ways, I will hear from Heaven, forgive their sins and heal their land."
2 Chronicles 7:14

DID YOU KNOW?

Seleucia is in modern day Iraq. It was one of the greatest cities in the world during this time.

Acts 13:1-5 Activity Sheet

Journey Of Shaul And BarNabba

These are some of the known places Shaul and BarNabba went to spread the Gospel. Draw a line to follow their journey. Start at Antioch in Syria.

1. Seleucia
2. Salamis
3. Paphos
4. Antioch (Pisidia)
5. Iconium
6. Lystra
7. Derbe
8. Attalia

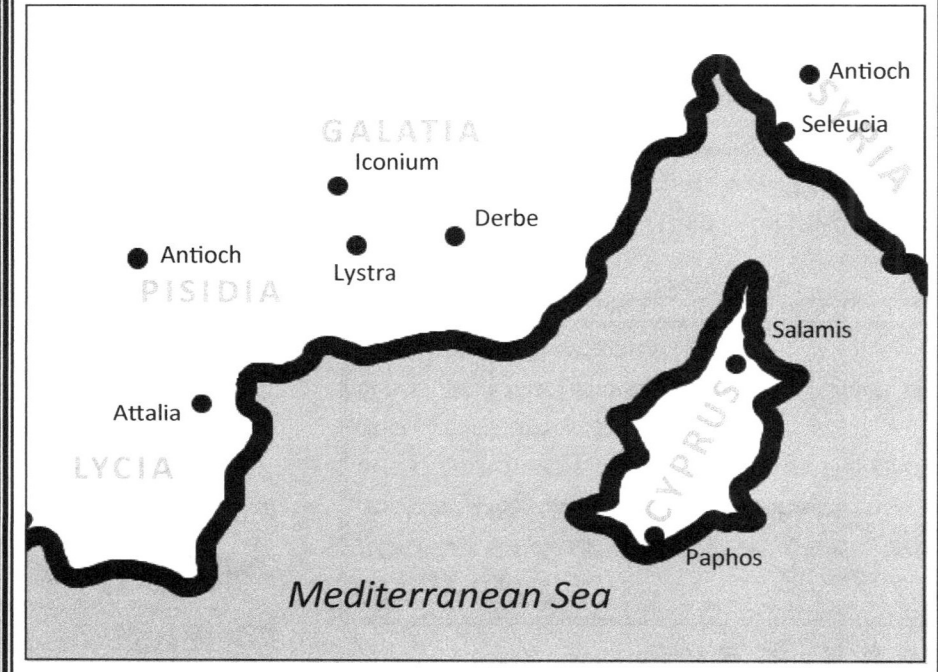

For an extension of this activity. Find this area on a modern day map. What are the places called today? Are they the same or different?

Shaul and BarNabba Anointed

"After fasting and praying, they placed their hands on them and sent them off." Acts 13:3

Sh'mini

פרשת שמיני

(Eighth) Leviticus 9:1-11:47

Parasha 26

Memory Verse

"They brought what Moshe [Moses] had ordered before the tent of meeting, and the whole community approached and stood before *ADONAI*."

Leviticus 9:5 CJB

Did You Know?

The Hoki fish has fins and scales when it is young, but when it gets older the scales fall off. What do you think? Is it clean or unclean?

STORY SUMMARY
ADONAI Comes Down: The people are instructed to sacrifice because ADONAI is going to appear. After the sacrifices and the blessing of the people, ADONAI comes down in the form of fire and consumes the burnt offering on the altar. Two of Aaron's sons do what has not been instructed and are instantly struck down.
Clean and Unclean Creatures: ADONAI gives a detailed list of animals and other creatures that are clean and unclean to eat.

WORD FOCUS
Kashrut: 'Food laws.' These food laws are based on this passage of scripture but can also have other considerations such as how the animal is treated.

MAIN MESSAGE
ADONAI made a way for His people to communicate with Him, but they needed to obey what He said. This was not because He was mean and vengeful but because He was so holy that anything unclean could not survive in His presence. Isra'el soon saw their need for a mediator between them and ADONAI. ADONAI is still looking for a clean people today. The food we put into our bodies is one way that we can become unclean.

KNOW ADONAI **OBEY** **BE SET APART**

Promise

Leviticus 10:3 CJB

"Through those who are near me, I will be consecrated, and before all the people I will be glorified."

Sh'mini Leviticus 9:1-11:47 Activity Sheet

Kosher

ADONAI gave categories of clean and unclean food. Can you find the unclean water creatures in the word search below?

NON-KOSHER SEAFOOD

```
B C L F X M I V Q Q X E T L S      CATFISH
A R P I N L K P X S R W C W N      EEL
U A C W E Y O K A R T L Y B W      PORPOISE
B B G Q E L L S E Q A W I L N      SHARK
K T E O L W G T N M X M K J O      WHALE
W I U A S O S R H S I F T A C      CLAM
D H C N A B E Z G F T M E C L      CRAB
U S A C O T R N F R O G J F N      FROG
D I X L S D P N Z A U Y H I H      LOBSTER
L I X Y E D A O R P M I R H S      OYSTER
D S O M W Y Q O T Y V H I I B      SCALLOP
E R G M Q H X K B D F B X X R      SHRIMP
G H P N K R A H S U M K J G P      SNAIL
Y X O F L A P O R P O I S E Q
U I M H C F Q G L O V Z V S J
```

Pig

"...The pig is unclean for you, because although it has a separate and completely divided hoof, it doesn't chew the cud." Leviticus 11:7 CJB

Sh'muel Bet

2 Samuel 6:1-19

Haftara 26 (Prophets)

Memory Verse

"So David and all the house of Isra'el brought up the ark of ADONAI with shouting and the sound of the shofar."

2 Samuel 6:15 CJB

Did You Know?

There are many kinds of natural laws such as, 'what goes up must come down.' In the same way, 'unholy not touching holy' is a natural law.

STORY SUMMARY

David Brings Home The Ark of ADONAI: King David arranges for the Ark of the Covenant to come back to Jerusalem. It is put on a cart pulled by an ox. The ox stumbles, and the ark nearly falls. Uzah tries to stop it and dies instantly. David can't understand why this has happened so He doesn't take the ark to Jerusalem. Meanwhile the family with the ark is being blessed. When David sends for the ark the next time he follows ADONAI's original instructions for moving it and rejoices with the people as they bring it home.

WORD FOCUS

Ephod: This was a garment worn by the priests. David wore one when he danced joyfully before ADONAI.

MAIN MESSAGE

ADONAI again shows how important it is to follow His ways. Nothing or no one unclean can touch the holy and live. ADONAI told Isra'el how to move the ark, but David didn't follow this. In a previous incident, people died just by looking at the ark (1 Sam 6:19-21). When David realised the mistake and made sure things were done right, he received joy from ADONAI that his heart could not contain. He didn't care about what people thought of him as he expressed this joy to ADONAI. With repentance and obedience comes blessing.

OBEY   **PUT RIGHT**   **REJOICE**

Promise

2 Samuel 6:12 CJB

"ADONAI has blessed the house of Oved-Edom and everyone who belongs to him, thanks to the ark of ADONAI."

Sh'muel Bet   2 Samuel 6:1-19 Activity Sheet

Joy

When you have the joy of ADONAI inside you it cannot be hidden.
Find the hidden articles in this pattern.

Apple   Book   Vase   butterfly   Hand   Flower

David Danced

"Then David danced and spun around with abandon before ADONAI, wearing a linen ephod." 2 Samuel 6:14 CJB

Acts 10 — B'rit Hadashah 26 (Newer Testament)

STORY SUMMARY

Kefa (Peter) has a Vision: Kefa sees many unclean animals coming down out of heaven on a sheet. ADONAI tells him to eat them. Kefa says, "No". He has never eaten anything unclean. ADONAI says that he is not to call anything unclean that ADONAI has made clean.

Cornelius is Baptised: Kefa realises ADONAI is talking about people not food. He meets Cornelius the gentile, who is then baptised along with his family.

WORD FOCUS

Mikveh: 'Immersion' or 'baptism' literally meaning 'a gathering of waters'. This was first used in B'resheet (Genesis 1:10). Mikvah, as a symbol of being spiritually cleansed, was a common practice, even before the time of Yeshua.

MEMORY VERSE

"...I now understand that [ADONAI] does not play favourites, but that whoever fears Him and does what is right is acceptable to Him, no matter what people he [or she] belongs to." Acts 10: 34-35 CJB

MAIN MESSAGE

Kefa knows that ADONAI is not talking about food in this vision. ADONAI had not called unclean meat clean. Kefa comes to understand that through Yeshua's sacrifice, people were no longer to be looked at as unclean. Yeshua had now become the pure sacrifice for anyone who accepted Him, such as Cornelius. We do not have to be a physical descendant of Abraham to be one of ADONAI's children.

PROMISE

"All the prophets bear witness to Him, that everyone who puts his trust in Him receives forgiveness of sins through His name."
Acts 10: 43 CJB

DID YOU KNOW?

Before the time of this vision, it was unacceptable for Jews to eat with non-Jews because they were seen as 'unclean'.

Acts 10 Activity Sheet

Clean and Unclean

Circle the clean animals and cross out the unclean animals.
There are 3 clean and 6 unclean.

"...He saw heaven opened, and something that looked like a large sheet being lowered to the ground by its four corners. In it were all kinds of four footed animals, crawling creatures and wild birds." Acts 10:11 CJB

Tazria

פרשת תזריע

(She Conceives) Leviticus 12:1-13:59

Parasha 27

Memory Verse

"We have all become like one who is unclean, and all our righteous deeds are like a filthy cloth..."

Isaiah 64:6 NRSV

Did You Know?

It seemed strange, but if the whole body was white with tzara'at then the person was pronounced clean! (Lev 13:13)

STORY SUMMARY

Being Unclean: Here ADONAI says what to do if someone has a baby, becomes sick with tzara'at (skin disease) or has clothes or other material that is mouldy.

WORD FOCUS

Tzara'at: 'a skin disease' often referred to as leprosy. However, leprosy as we know it today is different than the description given here. Tzara'at was recognised as a physical symptom of sin.

MAIN MESSAGE

Everyday life separates us from ADONAI, even if we cannot think of anything we have done that might be sinful. We come in contact with things all the time that are unclean. They are not necessarily sinful but maybe just unclean. On our own we are not able to please ADONAI. We need a saviour. Also, although not every illness is a result of sin, these illnesses and problems show, in a physical way, how untreated sin in our life and community can quickly spread.

BE CLEAN   **BE SAVED**   **BE SET APART**

Promise

Leviticus 12:8 CJB

"The *cohen* (priest) will make atonement for her, and she will be clean."

Tazria Leviticus 12:1-13:59 Activity Sheet

Sin

Sin will grow if we are not sorry for it. How many 4, 5 or 6 letter words can you think of that have the word sin in them?

4 Letters

S I N __

S I N __

5 Letters

__ __ S I N

__ __ S I N

S I N __ __

S I N __ __

__ S I N __

6 Letters

S I N __ __ __

__ __ __ S I N

__ __ __ S I N

S I N __ __ __

__ __ S I N __

S I N __ __ __

S I N __ __ __

S I N __ __ __

Mother and Baby

"...Such is the law for a woman who gives birth, whether to a boy or to a girl." Leviticus 12:7 CJB

Melakhim Bet

2 Kings 4:42-5:19

Haftara 27 (Prophets)

Memory Verse

"...I wish my lord could go to the prophet in Shomron! He could heal his *tzara'at*."
2 Kings 5:3 CJB

Did You Know?

The Yarden (From 'Yarad', meaning 'descend' or 'flow down.') is a river that flows between the Sea of Galilee and the Dead Sea. This is the same river Yeshua was immersed in. It is also known as the Jordan.

STORY SUMMARY

A Young Girl Helps her Master: Naaman, a respected commander of the king, is given a young Isra'elite girl as a servant for his wife. When the girl sees he has tzara'at, she tells his wife about Elisha the prophet, who could heal him. Naaman sets off to find him. When Elisha tells him to bathe seven times in the Yarden river, Naaman doesn't want to do it. He doesn't believe it will cure him. He eventually decides to do it anyway and is healed.

WORD FOCUS

Shabua: 'Seven', meaning to be 'full' or 'satisfied' or have 'enough'. This number in the bible is used a lot. The message it brings is completeness and holy perfection.

MAIN MESSAGE

Even though you are young, you can do amazing things for ADONAI. When you have strong faith and belief, others can see it. A seed of faith and hope can be planted in them. Also, you will be cleansed from your sin when you bring it to ADONAI and desire to do things His way. Sometimes it means stepping out in faith, even when you don't understand.

OBEY   **BE CLEAN**   **TRUST**

Promise

2 Kings 5:10 CJB

"Elisha sent a messenger to him, who said, 'Go and bathe in the Yarden [Jordan] seven times. Your skin will become as it was, and you will be clean".

2 Kings 4:42-5:19 Activity Sheet

Seven

Decode a hidden meaning of seven. Solve the sums to unlock the key to code.

7x1= ___ 7x2= ___ 7x3= ___ 7x4= ___ 7x5= ___ 7x6= ___ 7x7= ___ 7x6= ___

__ __ __ __ __ __ __ __

A	B	C	D	E	F	G	H	I	J
1	5	7	20	42	12	50	31	2	16

K	L	M	N	O	P	Q	R	S	T
46	35	21	6	14	28	10	18	24	49

U	V	W	X	Y	Y	Z
3	38	40	12	22	15	48

Naaman

"So he went down and immersed himself seven times in the Yarden, as the man of G-d had said to do; and his skin was restored and became like the skin of a child: and he became clean."
2 Kings 5:14 CJB

Luke 5:12-15

B'rit Hadashah 27 (Newer Testament)

STORY SUMMARY

Yeshua Heals: A man with tzara'at comes to Yeshua and begs to be cleansed. Yeshua cleanses him and sends him to the Temple to be cleared by the *cohen* (priest). The word spreads and many others come to Yeshua for healing. Yeshua is happy to heal these people but also needs time to be with ADONAI in prayer.

WORD FOCUS

Taher: 'Become clean', and **Raphe:** 'heal', have some similar meanings such as, 'become fresh' and 'purify,' but rapha also expresses ADONAI's desire to 'take care' of us as well as cleanse. It shows more of His heart towards us.

MEMORY VERSE

"'Sir, if you are willing, you can make me clean.' Yeshua reached out his hand and touched him, saying, 'I am willing! Be cleansed!' Immediately the tzara'at left him." Luke 5:12-13 CJB

MAIN MESSAGE

There is no sin too big for ADONAI to forgive if we are truly sorry. He wants us to be complete and restored, so we can live life as He planned. He is 'willing' and eagerly waiting to be asked. Also, it is very important we make time each day to spend with ADONAI in prayer. This is our power source for life.

PROMISE

"If we acknowledge our sins, then, since He is trustworthy and just, He will forgive them and purify us from all wrongdoing."
1 John 1:9 CJB

DID YOU KNOW?

Luke was not one of the twelve apostles. He was probably a gentile doctor. (Colossians 4:10-14)

Luke 5:12-15 Activity Sheet

Being Set Apart

ADONAI wants His people to be holy and cleansed. Separate these words into the right category of holy and unholy. Either rewrite them in the box or draw a line to the right box from each word.

clean   dirty   filthy   pure   detestable   good
lovely   abominable   noble   right   wrong   true
lies   slander   kind   mean   cruel   praise   sin

HOLY

UNHOLY

Yeshua Cleanses

"Once when Yeshua was in one of the towns, there came a man completely covered with *tzara'at*. On seeing Yeshua, he fell on his face and begged him, 'Sir, if you are willing, you can make me clean.'" Luke 5:12 CJB

Metzorah פרשת מצרע

(Person with Tzara'at) Leviticus 14:1-15:33

Parasha 28

Memory Verse

"The *cohen* purifying him is to place the person being purified with these items before ADONAI at the entrance to the tent of meetings."

Leviticus 14:11 CJB

Did You Know?

Vayikra (Leviticus) was ADONAI's instruction manual for His newly redeemed people. It showed them how to worship, serve and obey ADONAI in a way that was acceptable.

STORY SUMMARY

Law about Tzara'at: ADONAI tells Moshe (Moses) what to do if a person or a house has tzara'at.

Unclean Men and Women: ADONAI outlines some things that make men and women unclean to go into the Tabernacle. He gives instructions on these things.

WORD FOCUS

Kaphar: 'Atonement', meaning to 'carry away'. At Yom Kippur the sins were carried away from the people.

MAIN MESSAGE

ADONAI repeats a number of times, if atonement is made, the person will be clean. Adam and Eve's sin and curse has been passed down through every generation. Because of this we are all sinners, but ADONAI has been faithful in every generation to provide life and hope despite this curse. These laws all pointed to the time when the Messiah would come to take away the sin of the world. We will still suffer from the results of sin until all things are restored, but our personal restoration begins the moment we accept the atoning sacrifice of Yeshua on our behalf.

ATONEMENT **OBEY** **BE CLEANSED**

Promise

Zechariah 3:4 CJB

"'Take those filthy garments off him.' Then He said, 'See I am taking your guilt away. I will clothe you in fine robes.'"

PARENTAL NOTE: Discretion advised when using biblical narrative.

Metzorah Leviticus 14:1-15:33 Activity Sheet

Tzara'at

Can you spot the tzara'at in this house?
Each spot is represented by a **T**.
Circle the 10 **T**'s. They may be sideways or even upside down.

House

"When you have entered the land of the Kena'an which I am giving you as a possession, and I put an infection of *tzara'at* in a house in the land that you possess, then the owner of the house is to come and tell the *cohen*." Leviticus 14:34-35 CJB

Melakim Bet

2 Kings 7:3-20

Haftara 28 (Prophets)

Memory Verse

"But finally they said to each other, 'What we are doing is wrong. At a time of good news like this, we shouldn't keep it to ourselves.'"
2 Kings 7:9 CJB

Did You Know?

Just as tzara'at was a blessing in this story, house tzara'at was sometimes a blessing in Canaan. When house bricks were replaced, often Amorite treasure was found hidden in the old bricks.

STORY SUMMARY

Infected Men Save Isra'el: Jerusalem is surrounded by the army of Aram. There is a famine so everyone is hungry. Four men with tzara'at, who are outside the camp because they are unclean, decide to surrender themselves. They are amazed to discover that the army have fled because ADONAI caused them to hear what sounded like a mighty army approaching. The men eat and hide some things, but then think that they should share their find with Isra'el.

WORD FOCUS

Elisha: Meaning 'My G-d is Salvation'. Elisha was the prophet at the time of this story and came after Elijah (Eliyyahu), meaning 'My God is YHWH.'

MAIN MESSAGE

It is a long held view in Judaism that tzara'at was mostly a disease of greed. These four men were said to be connected with a man who had cheated Elisha in the past. Through this disease they had learned their lesson. Now they were able to be used by ADONAI to help save all Isra'el. They stopped themselves in their natural desire to hide the wealth for themselves and thought better of it. By sharing, they showed how they had changed. Sometimes we need to learn things the hard way but if we do learn, there are great blessings to be discovered.

REPENT   LEARN   SHARE   BE HUMBLE

Promise

2 Kings 7:1 CJB

"Elisha answered, 'Listen to the word of ADONAI. Here is what ADONAI says: Tomorrow, by this time, six quarts of fine flour will sell for only a *shekel*, and half a bushel of barley for a *shekel* at the gate of Shomron.'"

Melakim Bet 2 Kings 7:3-20 Activity Sheet

Elijah or Elisha

Who did the following things? Was it Elisha or Elijah? Look up the bible verse if you are unsure.

Who said: "How long will you waver between two opinions?"
1 Kings 18:21
ELISHA or ELIJAH

Who prophesied before three kings while a harp was playing?
2 Kings 3:13-16
ELISHA or ELIJAH

Who called down fire from Heaven?
1 Kings 18:36-38
ELISHA or ELIJAH

Who threw salt into the water springs?
2 Kings 2:19-21
ELISHA or ELIJAH

Whose father was Shaphat?
1 Kings 19:19-20
ELISHA or ELIJAH

Who did captain Naaman go to see?
2 Kings 5:10
ELISHA or ELIJAH

Four Men with Tzara'at

"Now there were four men with tzara'at at the entrance to the city gate, and they said to each other, 'why should we sit here till we die?'" 2 Kings 7:3 CJB

B'rit Hadashah 28
(Newer Testament)

Luke 8:43-48

STORY SUMMARY

Woman Healed: A woman who has been bleeding for many years reaches out and touches Yeshua's tzitzit and is instantly healed. Yeshua feels the power go out of Him and asks who has touched Him. Many people had been touching Him because He was in a crowd, but the woman confesses and Yeshua blesses her because of her faith.

WORD FOCUS

Tzitzit: 'Tassel'. This was commanded to be worn from the corner of the clothes to remember the instructions of ADONAI. (Numbers 15:38-39)

MEMORY VERSE

"But Yeshua said 'Someone did touch me, because I felt power go out of me'". Luke 8:47 CJB

MAIN MESSAGE

For many years this woman would not have been able to go to the Temple to worship because she was considered unclean. Because of her faith, she was healed and made clean. Yeshua wants to make us clean and take away what separates us from Him. If we really want Him and look for Him we will find Him.

PROMISE

"He said to her, 'My daughter, your trust has saved you; go in peace'". Luke 8:48 CJB

DID YOU KNOW?

Yeshua's ministry lasted three and a half years.

Luke 8:43-48 Activity Sheet

Just a Touch

Rewrite part of the passage in Luke 8:44-45 from the words in the box onto the fingers of the touching hands.

| touched | bleeding | asked | her |
| me | Yeshua | stopped. | "who |

Woman Touches Yeshua

"A woman who had had a hemorrhage for twelve years, and could not be healed by anyone, came up behind Him and touched the tzitzit on His robe; instantly her hemorrhaging stopped." Luke 8:43-44 CJB

Achrei Mot

פרשת אחרי מות

(After the Death) Leviticus 16:1-18:30

Parasha 29

Memory Verse

"...Tell your brother Aharon not to come at just any time into the Holy Place beyond the curtain..."

Leviticus 16:2 CJB

Did You Know?

There was a scarlet thread tied to the Az'azel (scape) goat that was said to have turned white when the Yom Kippur sacrifice had been accepted. It didn't turn white for 40 years before the Temple was destroyed in 70 CE.

STORY SUMMARY

Yom Kippur Instructions Given: ADONAI outlines the roll of the High Priest on Yom Kippur (Day of Atonement).

Rules For Sacrifices and Blood Given: ADONAI says the people are not to sacrifice to any other god or kill an animal for meat that is not first offered to Him. He also says not to eat blood.

Rules For Appropriate Relationships Given: ADONAI tells Isra'el who they cannot marry or form marriage-type relationships with.

WORD FOCUS

Az'azel: 'Scapegoat' or 'fallen angel'. Many believe the Az'azel goat represents Ha Satan. He will end up carrying the guilt when the forgiven sins are placed back on him.

MAIN MESSAGE

Although ADONAI forgave the sins of the people daily, the Temple had been made unclean and needed to be cleansed. The sin needed to be taken away from the Temple. Our sin costs life. This is why we are only saved by blood, because it has life. Also marriage is meant to be a blessing and a picture of the relationship ADONAI wants with us. When people join in unholy ways outside of ADONAI's plan it brings pain, not blessings, and confuses our picture of ADONAI.

FORGIVENESS   **CLEANSING**   **RELATIONSHIP**

Promise

Leviticus 17:11 CJB

"For the life of a creature is in the blood, and I have given it to you on the altar to make atonement for yourselves; for it is the blood that makes atonement because of the life."

PARENTAL NOTE: Discretion advised when using biblical narrative.

Achrei Mot Leviticus 16:1-18:30 Activity Sheet

The Two Goats

The only way the High Priest knew the difference between the two goats was by casting lots.
Circle the six differences between these two goats.

Az'azel Goat

"But the goat whose lot fell to Az'azel is to be presented alive to *ADONAI* to be used for making atonement over it by sending it away into the desert for Az'azel."
Leviticus 16:10 CJB

Yechezk'el

Ezekiel 22:1-19

Haftara 29 (Prophets)

Memory Verse

"...Then you will know that I am *ADONAI*."
Ezekiel 22:16 CJB

Did You Know?

Although Isra'el is now a nation again, many Isra'elites are still scattered among the nations.

STORY SUMMARY

Isra'el's Sins Exposed: ADONAI openly names all the evil things His people are doing and tells them how unhappy He is with them. They have not listened or obeyed and have broken their agreement with ADONAI. Because of their sins, they will be sent into exile and scattered among the goyim (nations). Then they will know that ADONAI is G-d.

WORD FOCUS

Goyim: Translated as either 'nation, people, gentile, heathen or another'. In exile, Isra'el was sent into the nations.

MAIN MESSAGE

This is one of the saddest passages in scripture. ADONAI's heart was aching over the sins of His chosen people. Being 'chosen' did not mean they were more special than anyone else, they were still capable of the same evil. Being chosen carried a responsibility not only to follow certain rituals, but to live a moral life and be a blessing to others. Even in their terrible sin, ADONAI showed mercy. His consequence was not a punishment but a 'STOP' sign to turn them around. Through the exile they would realise their sin and their need of Him. Then they would return. In hard times, we can often grow the most. We can also become more empathetic to others.

OBEY **LEARN** **RETURN**

Promise

Ezekiel 36:24 CJB

"For I will take you from among the nations, gather you from all the countries, and return you to your own soil."

Yechezk'el 22:1-19 Activity Sheet

Road Signs

Make it safely home by following the road signs.

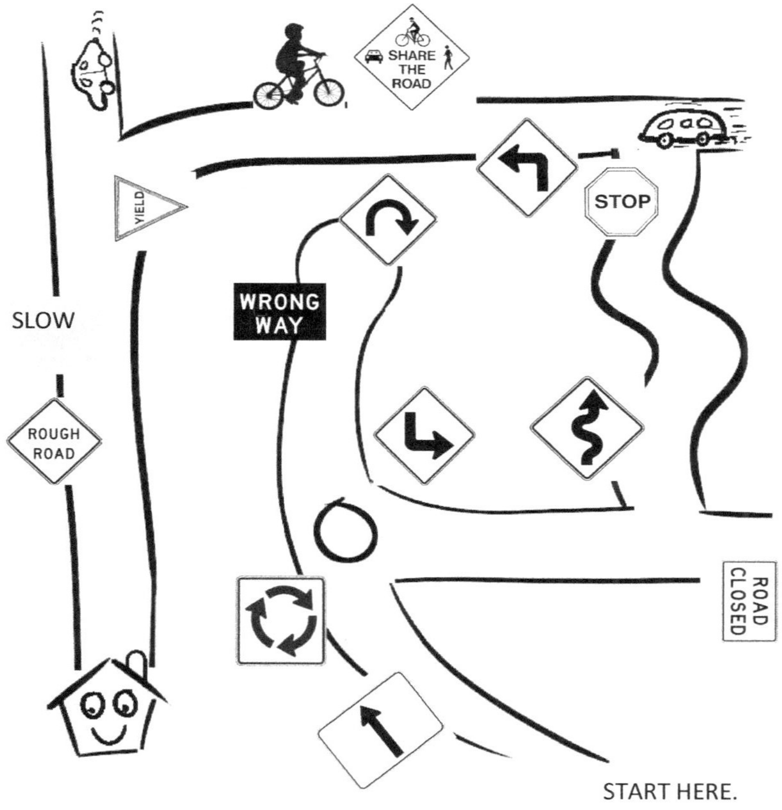

START HERE.

Return

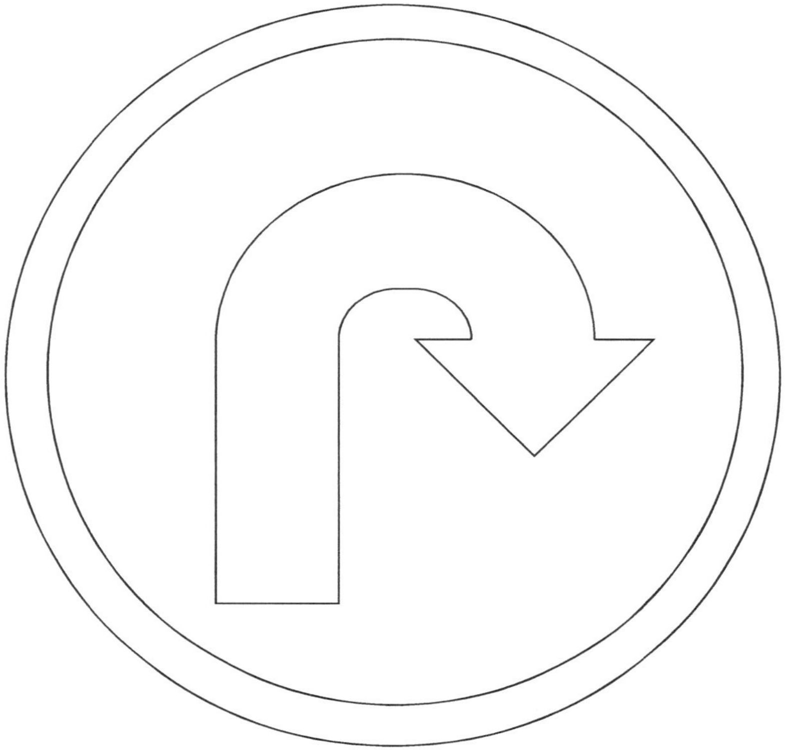

"Then if my people, who bear my name, will humble themselves, pray, seek my face and turn from their evil ways, I will hear from Heaven, forgive their sin and heal their land." 2 Chronicles 7:14 CJB

Hebrews 9:1-26

B'rit Hadashah 29 (Newer Testament)

STORY SUMMARY

Yom Kippur Explanation: Shaul (Paul) sets the scene by describing the Tabernacle and Yom Kippur (Day of Atonement) ritual. This system pointed to a time when Yeshua Himself became our High Priest, offering His own blood, as the perfect atoning sacrifice, in the Heavenly Tabernacle, for the sin of all. This one time act brings freedom to the forgiven sinner when their conscience is also cleared.

WORD FOCUS

Khakham: A person who knows the Torah or Talmud well.

MEMORY VERSE

"[ADONAI] presented [Yeshua] as a sacrifice of atonement, through the shedding of His blood, to be received by faith. He did this to demonstrate His righteousness, because in His [patience] He had left the sins committed beforehand unpunished." Romans 3:25 NIV

MAIN MESSAGE

The message of Yom Kippur is still relevant today. On Yom Kippur, instead of taking sacrifices to the Temple, we should think about what Yeshua has done for us as our High Priest. Leading up to this day, we are called to repent for our wrongs and be clean in the sight of ADONAI. Then our names will be written in the book of life. This desire for repentance should be natural as we remember the great cost of our sin and the atonement offered.

PROMISE

"How much more the blood of the Messiah, who, through the eternal spirit, offered Himself to [ADONAI] as a sacrifice without blemish, will purify the conscience from works that lead to death, so that we can serve the living [G-d!]"
Hebrews 9:14 CJB

DID YOU KNOW?

Shaul (Paul) was raised and educated by one the greatest teachers of his time, Rabbi Gamaliel.

Hebrews 9:1-26 Activity Sheet

Atonement

Earlier on we learn that atonement meant to 'cover over'.
Some of the letters in these words have been covered over.
Write the letters on the covers to reveal the passage.

S☐ a☐so th☐ Me☐siah, havin☐ b☐en of☐ered o☐ce t☐ be☐r ☐he sin☐ ☐f ma☐y wi☐l a☐pear a se☐ond ti☐e, n☐t to dea☐ wi☐h s☐n, b☐t to deli☐er th☐se w☐o a☐e eager☐y waiti☐g f☐r H☐m. Hebrews 9:28 CJB

Repentance

"You are not to do any kind of work on that day, because it is Yom Kippur, to make atonement for you before ADONAI your G-d."
Leviticus 23:28 CJB

Kedoshim פרשת קדשים

(Holy People) Leviticus 19:1-20:27

Parasha 30

Memory Verse

"...You people are to be holy because I, ADONAI your G-d, am holy."

Leviticus 19:2 CJB

Did You Know?

When they planted trees, they were not allowed to eat the fruit until the fifth year. ADONAI said the trees would bear more fruit if they followed this.

STORY SUMMARY
ADONAI Calls the Isra'elites to be Holy: Just as ADONAI is Holy, He wants His people to be holy. He lists some ways to be holy. The way they treat their parents, keep the sabbaths, worship, sacrifice, grow and harvest crops, eat their food, and treat others are all part of 'being holy'.

WORD FOCUS
Kadash: 'holy' or 'to sanctify/set apart or distinguish'. ADONAI doesn't want us, as His people, to look like the world. He wants us to look like Him.

MAIN MESSAGE
Being 'chosen' comes with responsibility. ADONAI wants His people to be different than others. We often fear we will be teased if we stand out, so we might want to be like the world. Especially when it seems we are the only ones who are different. ADONAI wants us to worship with others that believe in His ways too, so we can strengthen and support each other.

COMMUNITY **OBEY** **BE SET-APART**

Promise

Leviticus 20:24 CJB

"...You will inherit their land; I will give it to you as a possession, a land flowing with milk and honey."

PARENTAL NOTE: Discretion advised when using biblical narrative.

Kedoshim Leviticus 19:1-20:27 Activity Sheet

Being Different

There is a difference with one of these farmers, which sets him/her apart from the rest.

Circle the set-apart farmer.

Grapes

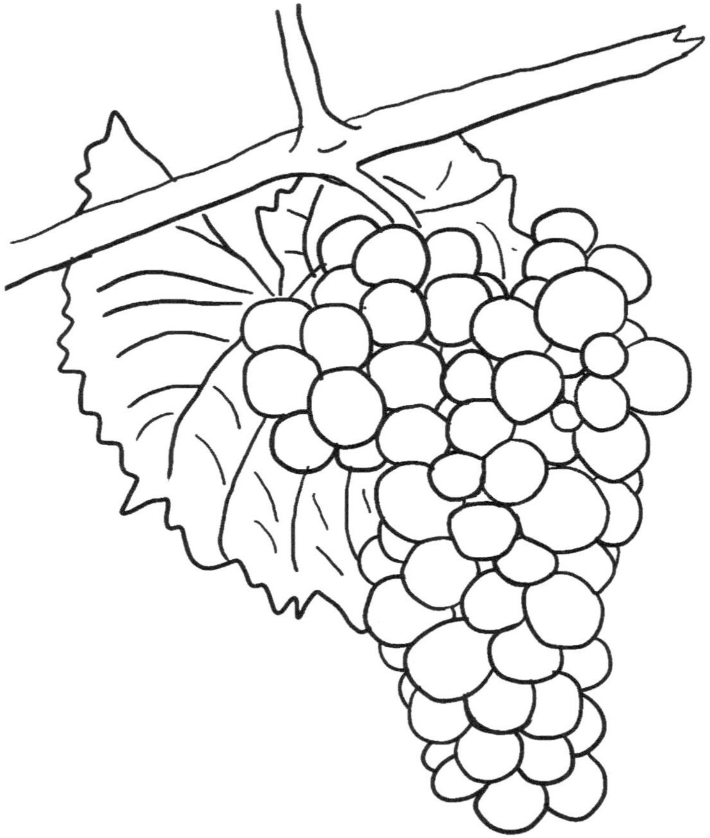

"Likewise, don't gather the grapes left on the vine or fallen on the ground after harvest; leave them for the poor and the foreigner; I am ADONAI your G-d." Leviticus 19:10 CJB

Yechezk'el

Ezekiel 20:2-20

Haftara 30 (Prophets)

Memory Verse

"'...Have you come to consult me? As I live,' says *ADONAI ELOHIM*, 'I swear that I will not let you consult me.'" Ezekiel 20:3 CJB

Did You Know?

Ezekiel was a prophet during the time of the seventy year exile in Babylon. The same time as Daniel.

STORY SUMMARY

ADONAI Reminds the Leaders of Isra'el's Rebellion: Through Ezekiel, the leaders come to enquire of ADONAI. Yet ADONAI refuses to be enquired of. Instead, He tells them of their sins. Not only their sin but that of their fathers and grandfathers before them. He would have dealt with them much earlier had it not been for His reputation among the nations.

WORD FOCUS

Elohim: Plural form of El meaning 'strong one.' It is used to describe G-d as the creator and judge of the universe and is the first name given Him in the bible.

MAIN MESSAGE

Just because something has been done for a long time, does not make it right. Traditions or practices passed down from our fathers, or their fathers, which are not in line with ADONAI's word, are not pleasing to Him. This passage goes so far as to say He won't even listen to our requests if we are not following His ways. Yet, as always, ADONAI doesn't leave us without hope. He doesn't wait for us to 'one day' choose Him. Instead He comes looking for us, to restore us, so His name will be honoured and His promises will happen. He will not be called a liar.

REPENT **PUT RIGHT** **OBEY** **HOPE**

Promise

Ezekiel 20:40 CJB

"'For on my holy mountain, the high mountain of Isra'el,' says *ADONAI ELOHIM*, the whole house of Isra'el, all of them will serve me in the land. I will accept them there...'"

Yechezk'el 20:2-20 Activity Sheet

Sin Spotting

The leaders didn't recognise their sin because it had become normal to them. Find and circle the 'sin' in these words. The first one is done for you.

Assas(sin)ate	Business	Criticising
Displeasing	Gutsiness	Disinclined
Insincere	Disinfect	Insinuate
Messiness	Misinform	Noisiness
Sinless	Accusing	Flimsiness

Out-Stretched Arm

"...I swear that surely with a mighty hand, with a stretched-out arm and with poured-out fury I myself will be king over you."
Ezekiel 20: 33 CJB

B'rit Hadashah 30
(Newer Testament)

Acts 15:1-21

STORY SUMMARY

Requirments for Gentiles: The apostles meet to discuss what regulations are binding for the new gentile believers because some people were saying they could only be saved if they followed certain practices. They agree that the law of ADONAI should not be something that is too hard for them to do. Four things they should follow were set: not to eat blood, food offered to idols, or meat that has been strangled. Also not to commit adultery. Other matters of the law they would learn in the synagogue on Shabbats in good time.

WORD FOCUS

Sh'eilah: A question about halakhah (Jewish Law) or tradition. This is the type of question they were discussing.

MEMORY VERSE

"It is through the love and kindness of the Lord Yeshua that we trust and are delivered—and it's the same with them."
Acts 15:11 CJB

MAIN MESSAGE

It is not by keeping the law that makes it possible to be saved. This comes as a gift of ADONAI when we put our trust in Him. The law is not for our salvation but to show us how to act if we want to call ourselves by His name. Different parts of the law are applied to different people and different times. Sometimes it is difficult to know what is expected of us today. The Ruach of ADONAI will guide us into all truth if we really want to know.

PROMISE

"After this, I will return; and I will rebuild the fallen tent of David. I will rebuild it's ruins, I will restore it, so that the rest of mankind may seek [ADONAI], that is all the Goyim (people) who have been called by my name, says *ADONAI* who is doing this."
Acts 15:16-18 CJB

DID YOU KNOW?

Some people use this passage to say that we no longer need to keep the Torah. Do you think these apostles were saying it is now alright to murder and steal? What else might it mean?

Acts 15:1-21 Activity Sheet

Grace

Help this lady lighten her heavy load. Use each letter once to find the answer to how we become saved. Cross out each letter after you use it, including those already done for you.

B__ g__ __ __ __
t__ __ __ __ __ __ __ __ f__ __ __ __

Spreading the Word

"In Iconium the same thing happened—they went into the synagogue and spoke in such a way that a large number of both Jews and Greeks came to trust." Acts 14:1 CJB

Parasha 31

פרשת אמור

Emor

(Speak) Leviticus 21:1-24:23

Memory Verse

"...I am to be regarded as holy among the people of Isra'el; I am *ADONAI* who makes you holy, who brought you out of the land of Egypt to be your G-d."

Leviticus 22:32-33 CJB

Did You Know?

Although a number of thoughts have been given, many scholars throughout history have been unsure of what the showbread in the Temple represented.

STORY SUMMARY

Instructions for the Priests Given: Continuing on the theme of 'being holy', ADONAI instructs the priests on more things they should and should not do.

ADONAI Sets His Calendar: ADONAI highlights His appointment times during the year.

Further Instructions Given: ADONAI gives instructions about the oil, lighting of the menorah, making the showbread and the penalty for using ADONAI's name as a curse.

WORD FOCUS- FEAST DAYS

Pesach: Passover
Chag HaBikkurim: Day of First Fruits
Shavuot: Feast of Weeks or Pentecost
Yom Kippur: Day of Atonement
Shabbat: Sabbath rest day
Chag HaMatzot: Feast of Unleavened Bread
Sefirat HaOmer: Counting of the Sheaves
Rosh Hashana/Yom Teruah: Feast of Trumpets/New Year
Sukkot: Feast of Tabernacles

MAIN MESSAGE

ADONAI has ways and times He wants to be worshipped. We don't always understand why, but as we learn to follow His ways, we begin to understand more. With every physical example He is trying to teach us about Himself and His plan for the world.

TRUST **OBEY** **BE SET APART**

Promise

Isaiah 62:12 CJB

"They will call them 'The Holy People, The Redeemed of *ADONAI.*'"

Emor Leviticus 21:1-24:23 Activity Sheet

Counting the Omar

There are 50 days in the counting of the Omar. Count until the 50th 'O' then write the seven letter word that comes next to reveal what comes on the 50th day.

S a h o d i a o y r o e w p y r o a f d j s b o v v a b v a d
h o s h f s d h u d o s b k s b l g d d o s b f d u i t i o e o
w h j v v k f y u o f u y a g a o l f v j h i j h y g g o e u y e
g o w e g o f j v o j b f i o f w i o g d f l d o s l b l i w f p o
d s k g f u w o f s d s k l o i g l x K l o g i f g f o t n e l l v v
o u i l g i g o i v b c v b z j b o i f g i g o v o c j h e g o u f
o g c o c o v j z k c v o a f g u y o u y c k o j v c o h j c v k
y f a g u g k v o k a k v o a k y u o g a u o g v u u k o k u
y o a r i f o n s h e y o w h e y s o w h e u d b o w h d o
r v n v o e u b s p d u r o s h a v u o t f u r w u c r a s t n

___ ___ ___ ___ ___ ___ ___

Yom Teruah

"In the seventh month on the first of the month is to be for you a day of complete rest for remembering, a holy convocation announced with blasts on the *shofar*."
Leviticus 23:23 CJB

Yechezi'el

Ezekiel 44:15-31

Haftara 31 (Prophets)

Memory Verse

"However, the *cohanim* (priests), who are L'vi'im (Levites) and descendants of Tzadok, who took care of my sanctuary when the people of Isra'el went astray from me— they are the ones who will approach me and serve me."
Ezekiel 44:15 CJB

Did You Know?

Ezekiel's temple has never been built.

STORY SUMMARY

The Priests Role in the Temple are Given: In vision, Ezekiel sees a future Temple where the Priests serve ADONAI. The description is very close to that given in Leviticus. However, there is one difference—these regular priests are given the instructions of the Levitical High Priest.

WORD FOCUS

Tzadok: 'Justice.' This was the name of the priest whose descendants would serve in the coming Temple. Tzadok was favoured because he stayed true to ADONAI when others rebelled.

MAIN MESSAGE

There is a time to come when ADONAI will be King and His people will be holy. His ways will be restored. Sometimes in this life, it seems wicked people get rewarded, but this shows us ADONAI sees our actions and reads our hearts. Our choices, whether good or bad, do not go unnoticed. In this life we may never see the results but if we are faithful, we will be remembered in the life to come.

OBEY **BE FAITHFUL** **HOPE**

Promise

Ezekiel 44:28 CJB

"Their inheritance is to be this: I myself am their inheritance."

Yechezi'el (Ezekiel) 44:15-31 Activity Sheet

Magnificent House

Ezekiel saw ADONAI's magnificent dwelling. Draw a house that you think would be magnificent.

Ezekiel's Temple

"They will enter my sanctuary, approach my table to minister to me and perform my service." Ezekiel 44:16 CJB

B'rit Hadashah 31
(Newer Testament)

Luke 23:53 - 24:8

STORY SUMMARY

Women Come to Annoint Yeshua's Body: Women who are followers of Yeshua watch to see where His body is laid and go to prepare spices and ointments. Because it is the day of rest, they wait until it is over to come back and anoint Him. They meet holy messengers who tell them Yeshua has risen.

WORD FOCUS

Yeshua: 'YHWH is Salvation'. This is a short form of YehoShua; Yeho meaning YHWH and Shua from Yasha, meaning to deliver, save or rescue. What a fitting name!

MEMORY VERSE

"The women who had come with Yeshua from Galil followed; they saw the tomb and how His body was placed in it."
Luke 23:55 CJB

MAIN MESSAGE

Leviticus 21 says priests were not to make themselves unclean by touching the dead. Because of this, it became a custom for women to prepare bodies for burial. Through their love and concern for Yeshua, even in His death, these women were rewarded by being the first ones to see Him alive.

PROMISE

"...Why are you looking for the living among the dead? He is not here; he has been raised..." Luke 24; 5-6 CJB

DID YOU KNOW?

Myrrh and aloe were the spices used to clean the body and to help with the smell.

Luke 23:53-24:8 Activity Sheet

Anoint

The women came to anoint the body of Yeshua. There are at least ten words that can be made from the word 'anoint'. Can you find ten? You do not need to use all the letters.

_____   _____

_____   _____

_____   _____

_____   _____

_____   _____

Risen

"But early the next day, while it was still very dark they took the spices they had prepared, went to the tomb, and found the stone rolled away from the tomb!" Luke 24:1-2 CJB

Behar

פרשת בהר

(On Mount) Leviticus 25:1-26:2

Parasha 32

Memory Verse

"...When you enter the land I am giving you, the land itself is to observe a Shabbat rest for ADONAI."

Leviticus 25:2 CJB

Did You Know?

Those who keep the Sabbath year of the land have said they get a lot more food in the sixth year, just as ADONAI promised.

STORY SUMMARY

Instructions for the Land Given: ADONAI tells Moshe the land is to have a rest every seven years and debts are to be forgiven. Every 50 years the land is to have an extra special yovel (jubilee) rest where it is to be given back to its original owners, and slaves are to be set free. He also tells them how to provide for the poor and reminds them not to worship idols.

WORD FOCUS

Yovel/Yubal: 'Rams Horn' 'Jubilee' or 'to be carried'. All of these relate to the meaning of Yovel. On the fiftieth year, starting on the Day of Atonement, they were to blow the rams horn to declare a year of Jubilee in which bondage and debt is carried away. Jubilee means to 'rejoice or be happy', also an 'anniversary'.

MAIN MESSAGE

This is ADONAI's ideal way to run a country, where the poor are protected, and greed has no place. It reminds the people that the land, and everything in it belongs to ADONAI, not to men. It also talks of a time where the slaves would be free and the land would return to its true owner.

HOPE   **PROMISE**   **FAIRNESS**

Promise

Isaiah 61:1-2 CJB

"The spirit of *ADONAI ELOHIM* is upon me, because *ADONAI* has anointed me to announce good news to the poor, He has sent me to heal the broken-hearted; to proclaim freedom to the captives, to let out into light those bound in the dark; to proclaim the year of the favour of *ADONAI*."

Behar Leviticus 25:1-26:2 Activity Sheet

Number Fifty

Numbers in the Bible represent things. Complete these sums. Circle the three words represented by the number 50.

2 x 25 =   Power

65 + 5 =   Judgement

2 x 20 =   time of testing

47 + 3 =   Deliverance

2 x 6 =   ADONAI's people

4 + 6 =   Restoration

10 x 5 =   Celebration

Year of Yovel

"...On *Yom Kippur* you are to sound a blast on the shofar, ...all through your land; and you are to consecrate the fiftieth year, proclaiming freedom throughout the land to all it's inhabitants. It will be a *yovel* for you." Leviticus 25:9 CJB

Yirmeyahu

Jeremiah 32:6-27

Haftara 32 (Prophets)

Memory Verse

"*ADONAI* G-d! You made heaven and earth by Your great power and outstretched arm; nothing is too hard for You."
Jeremiah 32:17 CJB

Did You Know

Yirmeyahu never went to Babylon like Daniel did. He was last heard from in Egypt.

STORY SUMMARY

ADONAI Tells Yirmeyahu (Jeremiah) to Buy Land: Yirmeyahu's cousin asks Yirmeyahu to buy his field, as ADONAI said he would. Yirmeyahu buys it legally. Then he praises ADONAI for being able to do all things. Jerusalem is about to be taken over by Babylon because of its sin. Yirmeyahu knows he will not be able to use the field but thanks ADONAI for the promise of hope.

WORD FOCUS

Shekel: 'Weight' used as money. Shekels weighed between 9-17 grams each. Commonly 11, 14 or 17 grams. If a shekel weighed about 14 ounces, then 2 shekels were about 1 ounce and 14 shekels were about 7 ounces. (1 ounce = 28.35g.)

MAIN MESSAGE

By instructing him to buy the land, ADONAI showed He was the owner of the land and His promises would happen. He gives a message of hope that one day the people will repent and return to the land. Today we are also looking forward to the 'Promised Land' and a time when Isra'el will return to ADONAI fully. This promise will happen just as He said.

TRUST **BELIEVE** **HOPE**

Promise

Jeremiah 32:15 CJB

"For *ADONAI-Tzva'ot,* the G-d of Isra'el, says that one day homes, fields and vinyards will again be bought in this land."

Yiremyahu (Jeremiah) 32:6-27 Activity Sheet

Shekels

This is a picture of an ancient Shekel.
Design your own coin in the spaces below.

Field in Isra'el

"So I bought the field at 'Anatot which belonged to my cousin Hanam'el and weighed out the money for him, seven ounces of silver shekels." Jeremiah 32:9 CJB

John 8:30-36 — B'rit Hadashah 32 (Newer Testament)

STORY SUMMARY

Yeshua Talks About Being Free: Yeshua tells the people they will be true Talmidim (disciples) and be free if they obey. The crowd is puzzled by the meaning because they are not slaves. Yeshua explains they are slaves to sin, but He can set them free.

WORD FOCUS

Talmid or Talmidim: 'Student', 'disciple' or 'taught one'. The root word comes from the letter 'lamed' which is the twelfth Hebrew letter. This is also symbolic of His people. It was the goal of the student to be like the teacher. Talmidim is the plural form.

MEMORY VERSE

"...Everyone who practices sin is a slave to sin."
John 8:34 CJB

MAIN MESSAGE

The physical freedom shown in the example of Yovel is a symbol of the freedom from sin found only in Yeshua. When we accept His sacrifice of blood we have power to live free of sin and death. If we are obedient, we can be taught and moulded, like clay, into His likeness.

PROMISE

"If you obey what I say you are really my *talmidim,* you will know the truth, and the truth will set you free."
John 8:31-32 CJB

DID YOU KNOW?

It was common for a talmid of a rabbi to give up everything to follow him because it was a great honour to be selected by a rabbi.

John 8:30-36 Activity Sheet

Free the letters to reveal what we must do to be free. Write them in the correct order in the spaces below.

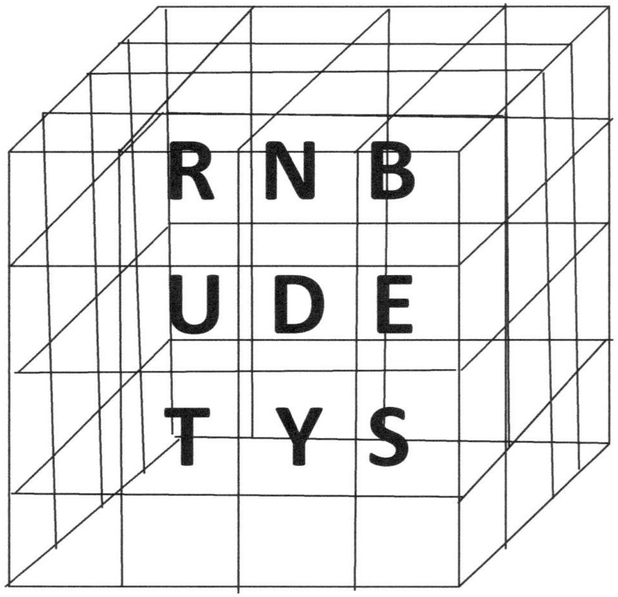

R N B
U D E
T Y S

T _ _ _ _

_ A _ _

O _ _ _

Freedom

" So if the son frees you, you will really be free!" John 8:36 CJB

Bechukotai
פרשת בחקתי

(By my Regulations) Leviticus 26:3-27:34

Parasha 33

Memory Verse

"Yet in spite of all that, I will not reject them when they are in the land of their enemies."

Leviticus 26:44 CJB

Did You Know?

Some people groups of the world today claim to be from the scattered tribes because their culture is similar.

STORY SUMMARY

Blessings and Curses Given: ADONAI tells the people about the good things that will happen if they follow His ways, and the consequences if they don't obey. He also gives hope by telling them about the forgiveness that will be given because of His promise with Avraham (Abraham). Then, ADONAI gives instructions for selling and redeeming.

WORD FOCUS

Chukat/Chuqqah/Hukath: 'Regulation', meaning something that is prescribed, an enactment or a statute. The ancient picture form is a wall with the sun rising, which shows something that is separated then brought back together by light. The light of ADONAI's ways helps bring us back together with Him after being separated by sin.

MAIN MESSAGE

Does this remind you of your parents? "If you do well, you can have a treat, but if you are disobedient there will be consequences." We don't like consequences, but they help us grow into the best person we can be. This is the same with ADONAI. He wants you to be the best you can be. History tells us that Isra'el disobeyed, but ADONAI has not given up on His people because He is a merciful father who keeps His promises. Because of Yeshua, redemption is available.

HOPE **MERCY** **FORGIVENESS**

Promise

Leviticus 26:3-4 CJB

"If you live by my regulations, observe my mitzvot (commands) and obey them; then I will provide the rain you need in its season."

Bechukotai Leviticus 26:3-27:34 Activity Sheet

Conditions

What did the people have to do to receive blessings?
Unscramble the words to find the answer.

PEKE _____

SHI _____

GSRLOETUNAI _____

Blessings

"...The land will yield its produce, and the trees in the field will yield their fruit." Leviticus 26:4 CJB

Yirmeyahu

Jeremiah 16:19-17:14

Haftara 33 (Prophets)

Memory Verse

"Heal me, *ADONAI*, and I will be healed; save me, and I will be saved, for you are my praise."
Jeremiah 17:14 CJB

Did You Know?

The land of Isra'el is not naturally fertile land, yet it is one of the largest exporters of fresh produce in the world.

STORY SUMMARY

ADONAI Seeks Trust: Yirmeyahu starts by praising ADONAI and then addresses the problem of the people. They are not trusting in ADONAI but trusting in their own efforts. They failed to keep the shmita (land sabbath) laws, and ADONAI compares this to idol worship. He finishes by again offering hope if they turn from their ways and put their trust in Him.

WORD FOCUS

Shmita: 'Release', referring to the seventh year when the land was to rest or have a 'shabbat' or 'sabbatical'. The land and the land owner were 'released' from their role of working to provide.

MAIN MESSAGE

Through the example of the shmita, ADONAI wanted to show His people that He was their provider, and everything came from Him. When they failed to follow this example, they also failed to trust in Him as their provider and began trusting in themselves. Sometimes when we work hard, it might seem we have done it on our own. We can forget how ADONAI provides for us or forget to thank Him for the talents He gives us. It is easy to say we trust in ADONAI, but our words need to be followed by actions.

TRUST **BELIEVE** **DO**

Promise

Jeremiah 17:7 CJB

"Blessed is the man who trusts in *ADONAI*; *ADONAI* will be his security."

Yireyahu 16:19-17:14 Activity Sheet

The Birkat Ha-Mazon

The Birkat Ha-Mazon blessing in Judaism has a number of different endings. Use these pictures to finish these blessings below.

Barukh ata ADONAI Eloheinu melekh ha'olam:

Blessed are You, Lord our G-d, Ruler of the universe, who brings forth/ creates:

1.  from the    _____   _____

2.  of the    _____   _____

3.  of the    _____   _____

4.  of the    _____   _____

Provider and Sustainer

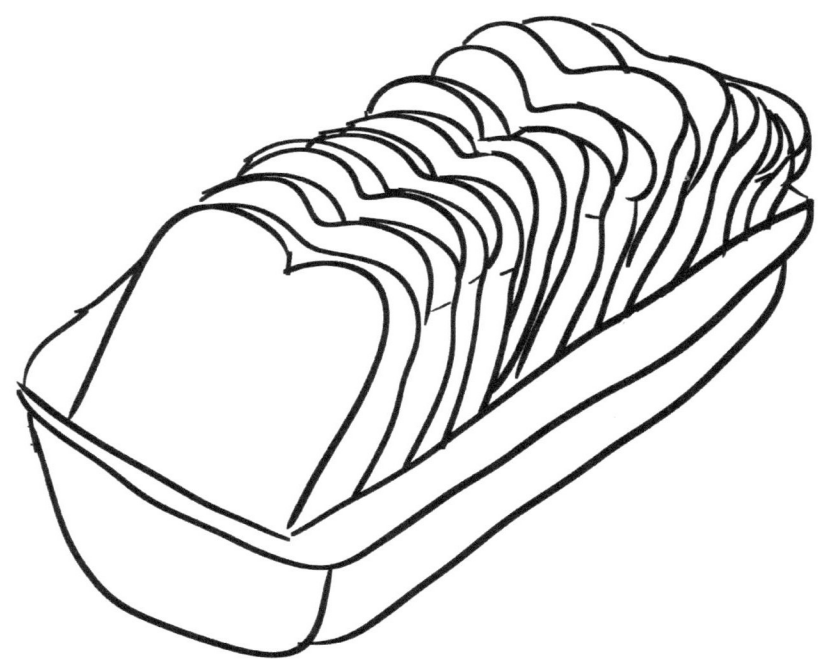

Barukh ata ADONAI Eloheinu Melekh ha'olam hamotzi lechem min ha'aretz.
Blessed are You, Lord our G-d, Ruler of the universe, who brings forth bread from the earth.

B'rit Hadashah 33
(Newer Testament)

John 14:15-21

STORY SUMMARY

Promise Of The Ruach HaShem Given: Yeshua tells His followers to keep His commandments, and He will bless them by asking the Father to send the Spirit of Truth to comfort and guide them. Yeshua Himself says He will come to them through this spirit of Truth.

WORD FOCUS

Ahavah: 'love' meaning 'I give'. This is an action word that describes what we do if we love. It is not a 'feeling' we have.

MEMORY VERSE

"If you love Me you will keep My commands."
John 14:15 CJB

MAIN MESSAGE

Yeshua is not teaching a different message than in the past. Leviticus 26:3-4 speaks a similar message of blessings for obedience. This 'rain in its season' is also understood to represent this giving of the Ruach HaShem (Spirit of G-d), which is a blessing given to those who obey.

PROMISE

"...And I will ask the Father, and He will give you another comforting counsellor like me, the Spirit of Truth, to be with you forever." John 14:16 CJB

DID YOU KNOW?

On Shavuot, the promise Yeshua gave was fulfilled.

John 14:15-21 Activity Sheet

Yeshua's Promise

In John 14:24, what did Yeshua say He would do for those who love Him? Unscramble the letters in the shapes to find out.

Ruach HaShem

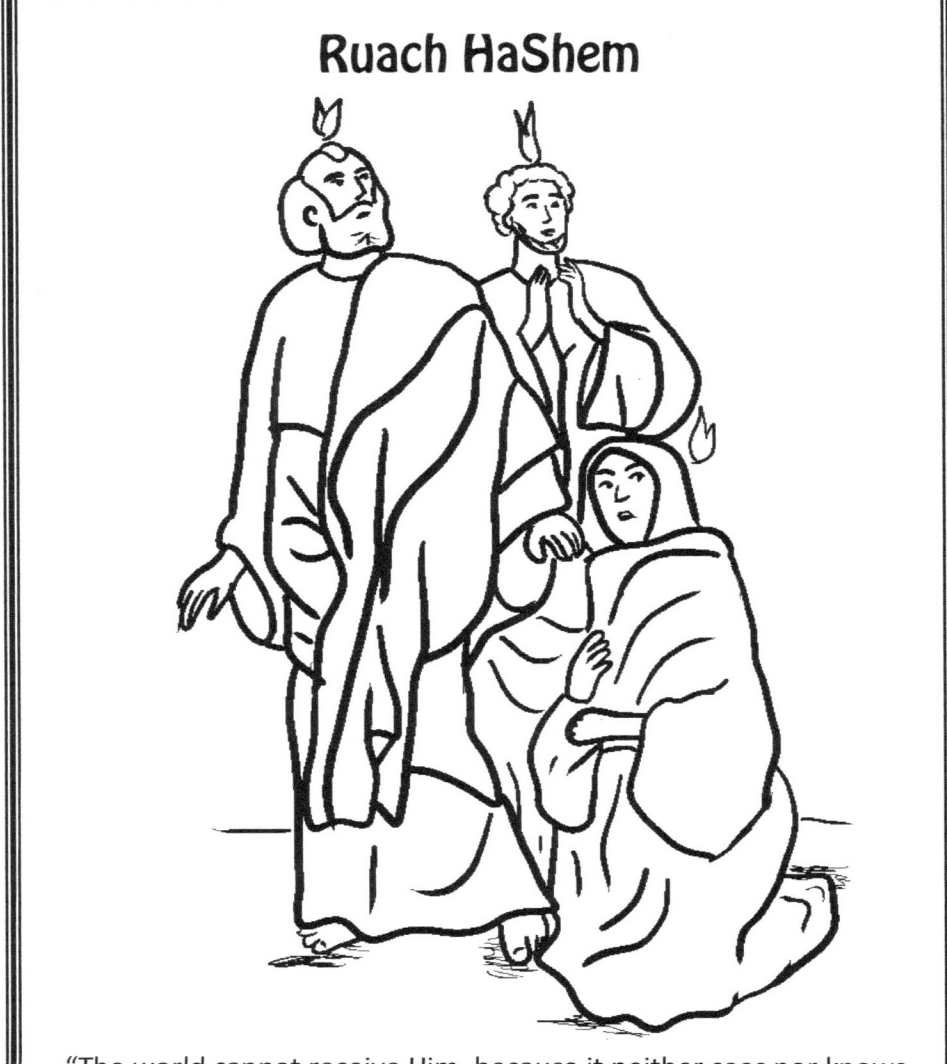

"The world cannot receive Him, because it neither sees nor knows Him. You know Him, because He is staying with you and will be united with you!" John 14:17 CJB

Shabbat Zachor — 1 Samuel 15:2-34

Haftara (Prophets)

Memory Verse

"For rebellion is like the sin of sorcery, stubbornness like the crime of idolatry. Because you have rejected the word of *ADONAI*, He too has rejected you as King."

1 Samuel 15:23 CJB

Did You Know?

Today is a special Shabbat to remember Purim. Haman, the Amalek descendant, tried to plot against the Jews but ADONAI saved them through Hadassah (Esther).

STORY SUMMARY

ADONAI Seeks to Avenge His People: ADONAI seeks Shaul's cooperation in His plan to fight for Isra'el and bring judgement on the Amalekites.

King Shaul's Disobediance: Because of King Shaul's greed, he does not follow ADONAI's instructions fully, and he keeps some things for himself. When Samuel the prophet tells Shaul of his sin, he makes excuses for his behaviour. ADONAI says Shaul will be removed as King.

WORD FOCUS

Tzvaot: 'Hosts' in a military term. Some translate it 'the Lord of Angel Armies'. ADONAI introduces Himself in this reading as 'ADONAI Tzvaot'. This shows His authority and intent to come as a warrior.

MAIN MESSAGE

ADONAI is prepared to fight on our behalf but often we have a role to play also. When we obey, His perfect plan can be achieved. It is important to know *why* we do things. Shaul used the sacrificial system as an excuse for his greed but ADONAI saw his true motive. If you have done something wrong, confessing it is more pleasing to ADONAI than making excuses and blaming someone else.

OBEY   **CONFESS**   **TRUST**

Promise

1 Samuel 15:22 CJB

"Sh'mu'el said, 'Does ADONAI take as much pleasure in burnt offerings and sacrifices as in obeying what ADONAI says? Surely obeying is better than sacrifice, and heeding orders than the fat of rams.'"

PARENTAL NOTE: Discretion advised when using biblical narrative.

ZACHOR 1 Samuel 15:2-34 Activity Sheet

Full Obedience

Half a picture is not a picture at all, just as half obedience is not obedience at all.

Complete the rest of the picture.

Samuel Anoints Shaul

"Samuel said to Shaul, "ADONAI sent me to anoint you king over His people, over Isra'el. Now listen to what ADONAI has to say." 1 Samuel 15:1 CJB

Shabbat Ha Gadol
(Pesach) Malachi 3:4-24

Haftara (Prophets)

Memory Verse

"...A record book was written in His presence for those who feared *ADONAI* and had respect for His name. 'They will be mine,' says *ADONAI-Tzva'ot*, in the day when I compose my own special treasure...'"
Malachi 3:16-17 CJB

Did You Know?

Yeshua died as our Passover Lamb. Passover is the best time to remember His death and resurrection.

STORY SUMMARY

ADONAI Tells of a Great Time to Come: Through Mal'akhi (Malachi), ADONAI promises to send Eliyahu (Elijah) in the future. Eliyahu will make ADONAI's people blameless. Wickedness would no longer be overlooked by ADONAI as it had been before, and it would be easy to see the difference between ADONAI's people and wicked people. To be a part of this promise, Isra'el is called to come back to ADONAI and start obeying His ways.

WORD FOCUS

Gadol: 'Great', is used in this verse to describe the day when Eliyahu will come and bring restoration.

MAIN MESSAGE

The Passover was a reminder of how ADONAI rescued His people and delivered them from bondage. It is also represents a time in the future when ADONAI will deliver the people again through Eliyahu. Because Eliyahu had already come, this person of Eliyahu referred to someone else like him. The B'rit Hadashah says John the Baptist was like Eliyahu, and it also says to expect Eliyahu at the end of time. Part of the Passover sedar is the expectation to see Eliyahu.

GRATITUDE   **HOPE**   **RESPECT**

Promise
Malachi 3:23 CJB

"Look, I will send you Eliyahu the prophet before the coming of the great and terrible day of the *ADONAI*."

Mal'akhi 3:4-24 (Pesach) Activity Sheet

Book Of Life

Fill in the blanks of the memory verse from Malachi 3:16 CJB.

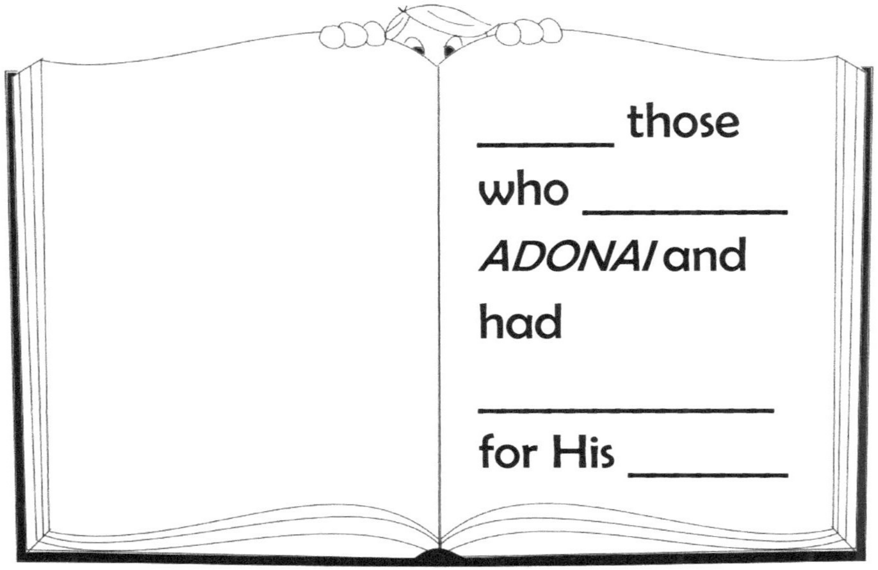

_____ those who _____ ADONAI and had _____ for His _____

Blood on the Door Frames

"They are to take some of the blood and smear it on the two sides and top of the door-frame at the entrance of the house in which they eat it." Exodus 12:7 CJB

THE BLOOD OF THE LAMB

At the first Pesach (Passover) ADONAI instructed the people to mark their doorways with lamb's blood so they would be spared from the plague of death.
Leviticus 17:11 helps us to understand why blood was needed. The people were then slaves in Egypt and needed to be rescued. Likewise, through sin we have all become slaves and we need to be rescued. The price of sin is death. Hebrews 9:22 tells us we cannot be forgiven without blood. Life is in the blood.
Do you want to pay for your sins with your own life? I don't, and ADONAI doesn't want us to either. He wants us to live. This is why He allowed the people in ancient times to kill an animal in their place.

The blood on the doorpost was a sign of faith on their part. They believed ADONAI and were willing to follow His instructions and accept the blood that was shed for them.

ADONAI told the people that they had to remember this time throughout their generations. Not only was this to be an important event for the people of that day, it was also to point to the future when the Messiah would come and shed His own blood.
John 1:29 and Matthew 26:28 identify Yeshua as this Messiah. When He was crucified, He shed His blood for us. Yeshua's death paid the price for those in the past and those who would come to trust Him in the future, as Romans 3:25 explains.

"For the life of a creature is in the blood, and I have given it to you on the altar to make atonement for yourselves; for it is the blood that makes atonement because of the life."
Leviticus 17:11 CJB

"For this is my blood, which ratifies the new covenant, my blood shed on behalf of many, so that they may have their sins forgiven."
Matthew 26:28 CJB

"...Almost everything is purified with blood; indeed without the shedding of blood there is no forgiveness of sins."
Hebrews 9:22 CJB

"Behold the Lamb of [ADONAI] who takes away the sin of the world."
John 1:29 CJB

"[ADONAI] put Yeshua forward as the kapparah [atonement] for sin through His faithfulness in respect to His [death through the blood sacrifice.] This vindicated [ADONAI's] rightousness; because, in His forbearance, He passed over, the sins people had committed in the past."
Romans 3:25 CJB

The lamb needed to be one they had cared for personally so they understood the cost. (Exodus 12:3)

Chametz (Leaven)

"For Seven days you are to eat matzah (unleavened bread) on the first day remove the leaven from your houses." Exodus 12:15 CJB

Why was this important? Was it really all about the bread?

1 Corinthians 5:6-7 explains "Your boasting is not good. Don't you know the saying, 'It takes only a little chametz (leaven) to leaven a whole batch of dough?' Get rid of your old chametz so you can be a new batch of dough..."

ADONAI was trying to teach the people a spiritual lesson through a physical example. The way they made bread was like sour dough today. The starter contained the chametz which made the bread rise. Before they baked the bread they would take a little of the mixture and keep it to make the next batch of bread so that the chametz would spread into the new batch, and it would rise. This is a great example of how sin can spread in our life. Have you ever seen someone break the rules and not get into trouble for it? Have you been tempted to think that maybe you could do it too? Can you see how that sin could spread?

By asking the people not to eat leaven for seven days, He was also asking them to think about the sin that might be in their lives and repent of it. Shaul (Paul) in the Corinthians passage above, goes on to say:

"..You are unleavened. For our Pesach lamb, the Messiah, has been sacrificed. So let us celebrate the seder not with leftover chametz, the chametz of wickedness and evil, but with the matzah of purity and truth." 1 Corinthians 5:7-8

This tells us that Yeshua has paid the price for our sin and encourages us to live free, in a way that pleases Him. When you eat matzah during this week, it is a great time to think about how you can live in purity and truth. What lies have you believed that might be making you or someone else unhappy? What truths can they be replaced with to turn that unhappiness into joy?

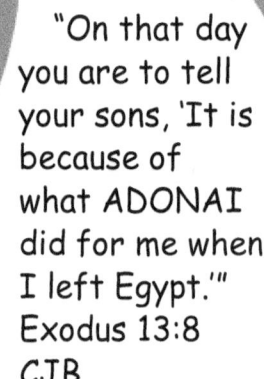

"On that day you are to tell your sons, 'It is because of what ADONAI did for me when I left Egypt.'"
Exodus 13:8
CJB

REDEEMED
PAID IN FULL

An important part of the Pesach (Passover) story is redemption, to be rescued by ADONAI or to be bought back. At Pesach, ADONAI redeemed the Isra'elites from Egypt. He passed over their houses and saved those inside. He then led them safely through the wilderness into their own land. This story did not end here. ADONAI is the God of yesterday today and tomorrow. This story has meaning to every generation. 1 Peter 1:18 tells us:

"..The ransom paid to free you from the worthless ways of life which your fathers passed on to you did not consist of anything perishable like silver or gold; on the contrary, it was the costly [blood sacrifice] death of the Messiah, as of a lamb without defect or spot."

When Yeshua came as the Pesach Lamb, this too was redemption. Egypt represented sin. It was this sin that Yeshua redeemed us from. We are no longer slaves to sin, but free in Yeshua, because He paid the price and has reclaimed us as His own. Now we are waiting for the day when He will come again and we will live with Him forever, as spoken of in Revelation 5:9-10;

"And they sang a new song, 'You are worthy to take the scroll and break it's seals; because You were slaughtered; at the cost of blood you ransomed for [ADONAI] persons from every tribe, language, people and nation. You made them into a kingdom for [ADONAI] to rule, cohanim (priests) to serve him; and they will rule over the earth.'"

TEST YOUR PESACH KNOWLEDGE
Test Your Pesach Knowledge

Complete the crossword below

Across
2. Yeshua paid for the sin of the _____ with His own blood
3. Hebrew word for Passover.
5. Without _____ there is no forgiveness of sin.
10. the story of Pesach is the story of _____
11. Pesach is on the 15th day of the _____ month
12. Leaven represents _____
13. Yeshua will _____ His people out of the world.

Down
1. Matzah represents purity and _____ and without blemish.
4. The lamb had to be _____ and without blemish.
6. Hebrew word for unleavened bread
7. Yeshua redeemed _____ out of sin.
8. Adonai redeemed Israel out of _____
9. English word for Hametz

LEAVING EGYPT

PSALMS 118:24
"This is the day that ADONAI has made. Let us rejoice and be glad in it."

69

The Pesach Seder Plate

Karpas— Exodus 1:7 Parsley or celery. A symbol of spring and new life for Isra'el, and the hyssop used to sprinkle the blood on the door posts. This is dipped in saltwater to symbolize the tears of being in slavery.

Maror— Exodus 1:13-14 Bitter lettuce, dandelion or endive (maror) and horseradish (chazeret). These represent the bitterness of the hardship of slavery.

Zero'a— Exodus 12:13 A Lamb shank bone, representing the blood of the innocent lamb that was painted on the doorposts to save Israel. Yeshua became the perfect Pesach lamb and was also the outstretched arm of ADONAI sent to save.

Charoset

Exodus 1:13-14 An apple, fruit of the vine and nut mix representing the hard labour of making bricks in Egypt. Yet even hard times can be sweet when rescue is near.

Matzah Bread

Exodus 12:15-20 Made without leaven and with Pesach-kosher flour. Three sheets of matzah are covered and set aside for the leader.

Beitzah— Roasted egg, to remember the roasted daily sacrifice at the temple. Yeshua became this sacrifice.

Salt Water Bowel Exodus 1:23-25 This is not usually on the plate, but on the side.

Parasha 24

Across
3. Grain
4. Sin

Down
1. Burnt
2. Peace
3. Guilt

Haftara 24

B'rit Hadasha 24 DOVE

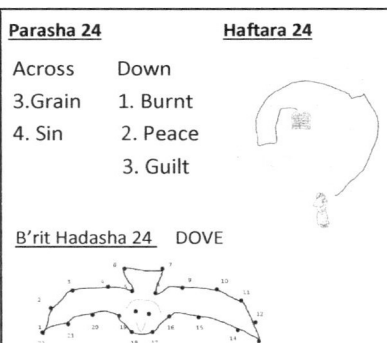

Parasha 25

Behold | Tent door | See

Haftara 25

B'rit Hadasha 25

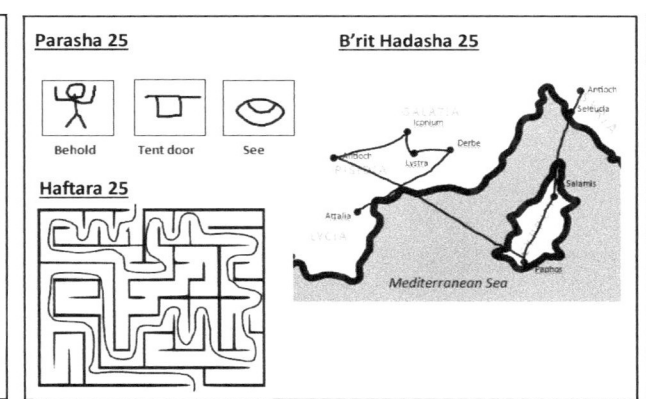

Parasha 26

NON-KOSHER SEAFOOD

CATFISH, EEL, PORPOISE, SHARK, WHALE, CLAM, CRAB, FROG, LOBSTER, OYSTER, SCALLOP, SHRIMP, SNAIL

Haftara 26

Apple, Book, Vase, butterfly, Hand, Flower

B'rit Hadashah 26

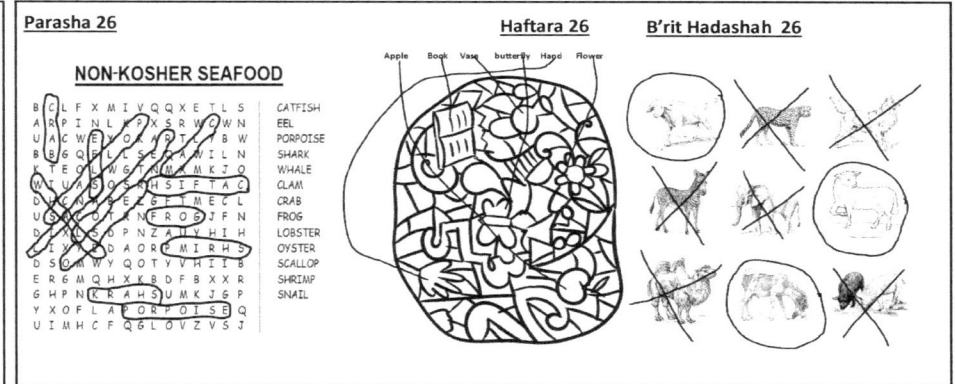

Parasha 27

(your own answers may vary)

4: Sink, Sing 5: Resin, Basin, Sinus, Using. 6: Single, Cousin, Raisin, Singer, Rising, Sinner, Sinned, Sinful

Haftara 27

7x1=7=C, 7x2=14=O, 7x3=21=M, 7x4=28=P, 7X5=35=L, 7x6=42=E, 7X7=49=T, 7X6=42=E

B'ritHadashah 27

Holy= clean, pure, good, lovely, noble, right, true, kind, praise.

Parasha 28

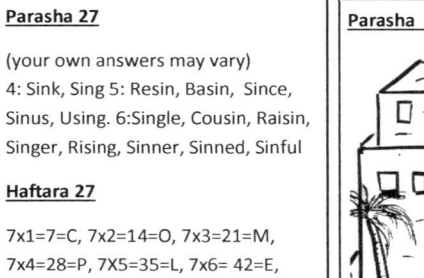

B'rit Hadashah 28

touched me | bleeding Yeshua | asked stopped. | her who

Haftara 28

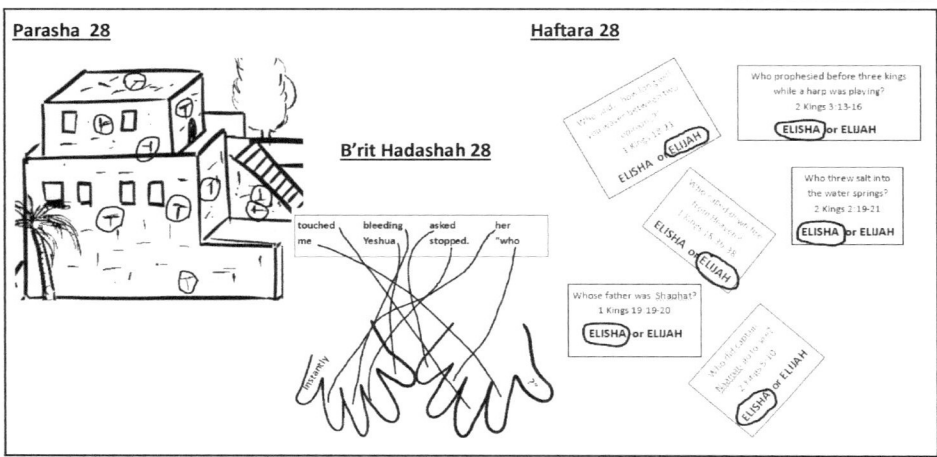

Parasha 29

Haftara 29

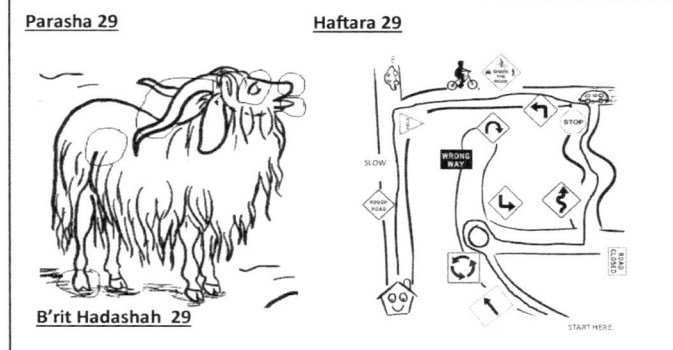

B'rit Hadashah 29

So also the Messiah having been offered once to bear the sins of many will appear a second time, not to deal with sin, but to deliver those who are eagerly waiting for Him.

Parasha 30

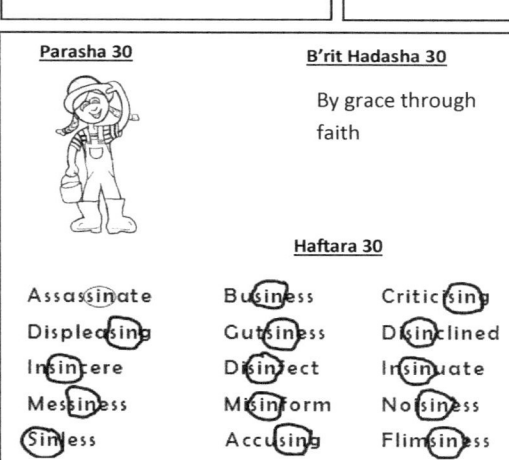

B'rit Hadasha 30

By grace through faith

Haftara 30

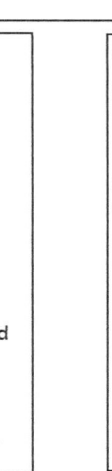

Assassinate, Business, Criticising, Displeasing, Gutsiness, Disinclined, Insincere, Disinfect, Insinuate, Messiness, Misinform, Noisiness, Sinless, Accusing, Flimsiness

Parasha 31

Shavuot

B'rit Hadashah 31

no, in, ant, on, to tin, ton, tan, not, it

Parasha 32

Power, Deliverance, Celebration

Haftara 32

TRUST AND OBEY

Parasha 33

KEEP HIS REGULATIONS

Haftara 12

Bread, earth
Fruit, vine
Fruit, tree
Fruit, earth

B'rit Hadasha 33

Reveal Himself to them

Shabbat Zachor

Shabbat Ha Gadol

For those who feared ADONAI and had respect for His name.

Pesach Special

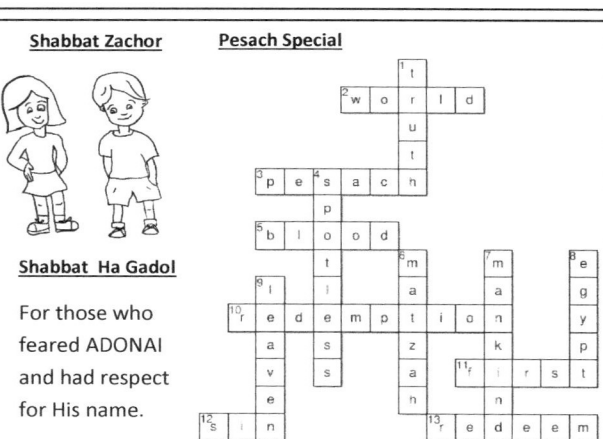

Answers

References and websites used
In order of appearance

reformjudaism.org

templeinstitute.org

funtrivia.com

Torah.org

Brad Scott Episode 3 Yahtube

Richard Elofer

behindthename.com

Stock image

theworkofgodschildren.org

bible.org

coolnotions.com

Narrow-gate.net

Freepik.com

Examiner.com

Scrabblefinder.com

Morgue files

ancient-hebrew.org

aish.com

Clal.org

Israelect.com

Plaza1.net

Wildbranch.org

www.ingramcontent.com/pod-product-compliance
Lightning Source LLC
LaVergne TN
LVHW081449070426
835507LV00018B/2057